•50

•51

•75

•118

•117

•119

•52

•116

•120

•64

•65

•74

•63

•70

•122

•66

•68 71

•69

•72

•123

•73

•113

•114

•67

•126

•127

•125

•129

135

•128

•130

134•

132

•133

124

•131 •136

•138

•115

•139

•89

•140
•141

•88

•142

•90

•143

•91

•98

•146

92•

93

•99

95

96

100

147

97

•102

144

•94

101

•104

•145

•105

•148

•103

150

•107

•106

•149

•151

•110

154

•153

•152

•111

•155

•156

•158

•157

•164

•161

•163

•159

•160

•162

OUR MAGNIFICENT WILDERNESS

40 OF THE GREATEST NATURAL WORLD HERITAGE SITES

Our Magnificent Wilderness
Claes Grundsten and Peter Hanneberg

Copyright © Claes Grundsten and Peter Hanneberg 2000
Text copyright © Claes Grundsten and Peter Hanneberg 2000
Artwork and map copyright © Claes Grundsten and Peter Hanneberg 2000
For copyright of photographs see page 224 which is to be
regarded as an extension of this copyright

First published in Sweden in 2000 by
Bokförlaget Max Ström

10 9 8 7 6 5 4 3 2 1

Translated by Julie Martin in association with
First Edition Translations Ltd, Cambridge, UK

This edition published in 2002 by
Duncan Baird Publishers Ltd
Sixth Floor
Castle House
75–76 Wells Street
London W1T 3QH

Managing Editor: Christopher Westhorp
Editor: Ingrid Court-Jones
Designers: Daniel Back, with additional design work for this edition
by Joy Wheeler and Dan Sturges
Map artwork: Martin Thelander

British Library Cataloguing-in-Publication Data:
A CIP record for this book is available from the British Library.

ISBN: 1-903296-77-3

10 9 8 7 6 5 4 3 2 1

Typeset in Bembo
Colour reproduction by Colourscan, Singapore
Printed and bound in Singapore by Imago
Printed on Stora Enso's 130 gsm Multi Art Matt

OUR MAGNIFICENT WILDERNESS

40 OF THE GREATEST NATURAL WORLD HERITAGE SITES

DUNCAN BAIRD PUBLISHERS

LONDON

Claes Grundsten and Peter Hanneberg

FOREWORD

BY THE DIRECTOR-GENERAL OF UNESCO

The year 2002 is the 30th anniversary of the Convention concerning the protection of the world's cultural and natural heritage, adopted by the General Conference of UNESCO in 1972. This important event is not only an occasion to celebrate but also to strongly reaffirm the World Heritage Convention's mission of preserving our world's natural and cultural heritage for future generations.

Its focus on both natural and cultural heritage makes the World Heritage Convention a unique legal instrument. This close link between nature and culture is expressed through the Emblem's interwoven design: A central square symbolizes the priceless treasures created by humanity, while a globe encircles the earth's invaluable natural heritage. Above all, the Emblem represents the universal values for which the Convention stands.

World Heritage sites constitute a common heritage to be treasured as unique testimonies to the enduring past and to the complexity and mystery of the world's incalculable environmental riches. Their disappearance would be an irreparable loss for each and every one of us.

And yet, to varying degrees, most of these sites face threats and difficult management challenges.

The preservation of our common heritage concerns us all. The outstanding values of these sites must be preserved for all humanity; preserved through a closer co-operation among nations and by ensuring the support needed to the dedicated individuals charged with the day-to-day responsibility of their protection and conservation.

This book is a tribute to some of our most well-known Natural World Heritage Sites. It is my hope that the beautiful photographs and inspiring text will enlighten even more people about UNESCO's World Heritage Convention and its immense importance to the safeguarding of our shared World Heritage.

Koïchiro Matsuura

CONTENTS

WORLD HERITAGE —

ON THE WORLD HERITAGE LIST AT UNESCO, ONE OF THE UN AGENCIES, there are many of the Earth's finest sites and those most deserving of protection. In recent years we have had the privilege of being able to stay in about forty of them, spread over six continents. To begin with we traveled for our own sakes, independently of each other, driven by curiosity and the joy of discovery. Gradually our travels turned into a project to communicate our impressions of these magnificent and precious places to a wider public. Our aim in the selection featured in this book is to try to disseminate a knowledge of and feeling for the Earth's fascinating natural, geographical, and biological diversity. We would also like to encourage people to visit these areas themselves, but such travels require a responsible attitude and a strict observance of the ethical rules of ecotourism.

The World Heritage Convention has created an interesting link that binds together many of these distinctive natural sites into a global and more palpable network. In this way the Earth's scientific and esthetic conservation assets attract greater significance and attention. Through the involvement of the UN a clearer connection is also made between humanity's desire for peace and its need for a sound natural world. The World Heritage Convention entails the rich countries helping the poor ones to preserve their world heritage, coordinated through a special World Heritage Fund. The UN Educational, Scientific, and Cultural Organization (UNESCO) also has another system, Man and the Biosphere Program, which designates valuable areas as biosphere reserves. Some of these coincide with the World Heritage sites (see the list on page 225).

The World Heritage list is based on the Convention for the protection of the world's cultural and natural heritage, which was adopted by UNESCO in 1972. Since then 167 countries have subscribed to the Convention. The first twelve World Heritage sites were registered in 1978, namely the four national parks of Yellowstone in the USA, the Galápagos Islands in Ecuador, Nahanni in Canada, and Simen in Ethiopia, plus eight cultural sites. In December each year a number of new sites have been adopted, from seven in 1989 to thirty-one in 2001. At the time of going to press there is a total of 721 World Heritage sites, of which 144 are natural, 554 cultural, and twenty-three a mixture of the two.

In order to be designated as natural or cultural heritage, a site must live up to the criterion of "outstanding universal value." The World Conservation Union (IUCN) scrutinizes a country's nominations for natural heritage and the International Council on Monuments and Sites (ICOMOS)

THE INHERITANCE
OF THE FUTURE

those for cultural heritage, after visiting the sites. Their assessments are then reviewed by the World Heritage Office, after which the nominations reach the World Heritage Committee for a decision in December of the year in question.

In the data section accompanying each entry we have cited the grounds for the decision on heritage status. Such a decision requires that at least one of the following criteria should be met:

I GEOLOGY: outstanding example of visible development stages in the history of the Earth, ongoing formation of natural features or significant geological structures in the landscape.

II ECOLOGY: outstanding example of ongoing ecological and biological processes developing plant and animal communities and ecosystems on land, in freshwater, coastal waters, and the sea.

III NATURAL BEAUTY: outstanding natural phenomenon or landscape of exceptional natural beauty.

IV THREATENED SPECIES: important natural environments that can protect biological diversity, including threatened species of outstanding universal value to research and nature conservation.

IN SPITE OF THE INTERNATIONAL PROTECTION implied by entry on the World Heritage list, serious threats sometimes arise to the sites selected. A separate list has been drawn up of threatened natural heritage sites, and there are eighteen on the list today. The threats may consist of deficiencies in management, tourism, poor infrastructures for waste and drainage, acts of war, invasion by alien species, plans for exploitation, water control, road-building, mining, animal and plant diseases, poaching, migration of peoples, livestock, pollution, or earthquakes.

For many of UNESCO's natural heritage sites timelessness is a common denominator. The qualities of each place have been developed over a very long period. Likewise they need to be cared for with a view to the distant future so that successive generations can inherit our investment and enjoy the yield from this magnificent capital. It is our hope that this book will create the will among its readers to get to know these sites and, as a result of that knowledge, to contribute to their protection. We who are alive today have a responsibility to manage this wealth for future generations.

Stockholm, January 2002
The authors

NORTH AMERICA

North America extends from the Arctic to Mexico, where a natural geographical boundary is formed with the tropics of Central and South America. From Alaska in the north to Arizona in the south, the Rocky Mountains stretch out like a beam supporting the whole subcontinent. To the west lie hot desert plateaus and a mild coastal strip; to the east, flat prairies and deciduous forests; in the southeast, Florida's wetlands; and in the north, pine forests and Arctic tundra. Most heritage sites have been selected primarily for their geological value and natural beauty, but ecological significance has also been taken into account. In order to describe this diversity we have ventured deep into the Grand Canyon, beneath the giant trees on the west coast, above the precipices of Yosemite, onto the majestic massifs of Canada's Rocky Mountains, and among the hot springs of Yellowstone. We have also encountered North America's rich animal life in the Rockies and the Everglades.

1. YELLOWSTONE, USA
2. REDWOOD, USA
3. THE ROCKY MOUNTAINS, CANADA
4. WATERTON GLACIER, CANADA–USA
5. YOSEMITE, USA
6. GRAND CANYON, USA
7. EVERGLADES, USA

YELLOWSTONE
—THE MOTHER OF ALL NATIONAL PARKS

In June, cutthroat trout jump the falls in LeHardy Rapids, anxious to reach their breeding grounds.

The wild Lower Falls hurls itself down into Yellowstone's Grand Canyon, whose yellow rocks have given the river and the national park their name.

THE ABSAROKA RANGE IN THE ROCKIES, just east of the North American continent's watershed, is where the magical Yellowstone River is born. In small cascades it tumbles down into the Yellowstone National Park and lingers a while in the 20-mile (30km) wide waters of the Yellowstone Lake, safely watched over by around ten 11,500-foot (3,500m) high sentinels with snow on their crowns. North of the lake the river meets LeHardy Rapids and soon after disappears over two vertical falls with a total drop of 422 feet (129m). Once down in the Yellowstone, it continues on between yellow and orange walls, around Mount Washburn and meets the Tower Creek tributary, which falls from a fortress of towers and pinnacles. It cuts through a plateau, leaves the national park and turns east, seeking the Missouri River that will carry it to the sea.

It was over 120 years ago that the first artists found their way here and on the heart-stopping bluff that became known as Artist Point, immortal masterpieces in oil were created, depicting the fiery ravine and Yellowstone Lower Fall.

It was a heady experience for members of General Washburn's expedition in 1870 to hear the nearby falls when they set up camp at Cascade Creek. Nathaniel Pitt Langford, later known as "National Park" Langford, recorded in his diary that he was "so confused" by his impressions—and described his "inability to cope with or even comprehend the mighty architecture of nature. More than all this I felt as never before my entire dependence on the Almighty Power who had wrought these wonders."

The canyon provided the expeditionaries with vivid experiences of beauty tinged with fear. The walls of the ravine are dizzyingly high and consist of weathered volcanic rock in shades of yellow and red. As one of the first visitors, and moreover a devout Christian, it was undoubtedly easy for Pitt to be overcome by visions of hell, particularly as even today vapors still rise from below ground.

In 1900, thirty years after Washburn, the legendary natural historian John Muir wrote that Mother Earth, wherever in the world one meets her, always seems familiar. "But here the very ground is changed, as if belonging to some other world … . All the earth hereabouts seems to be paint."

Yellowstone Lake, the highest mountain lake in the USA at an altitude of over 7,700 feet (2,300m), lies without a ripple on a crystal morning. A few anglers on the shore are

Mammoth Hot Springs is known for its natural sculptures of crystallized calcium carbonate.

A moose grazes on grass sprouting where the great forest fires raged in 1988.

Ferrous compounds color Sunset Spring a rusty red.

Following pages: Tower Fall was named for the rock pinnacles above the falls.

casting for lake trout and pierce the mirror-like surface. Most of the fish are introduced species, which have largely driven out the native cutthroat trout.

A bison stands at the water's edge in Mary Bay and poses against the majestic backdrop of the Absaroka Range, a sight from Buffalo Bill's era. How good it feels to know that this buffalo has survived the ignorance of that period. Bison were once shot for hides and meat, but undoubtedly just for sport in the main. If any hunt in the world ever lacked both morality and common sense it was the white man's slaughter of the bison in nineteenth-century America.

In 1805 the legendary Meriwether Lewis wrote in his diary: "I determined to encamp on the banks of the Yellowstone River ... the whole face of the country was covered with herds of Buffaloe, Elk and Antelopes." His traveling companion William Clark noted "great numbers of Buffalow in every direction. I think about ten thousand may be seen in a view."

Setting up the national park in 1872 helped to stem the senseless slaughter and save the species. However, poaching continued in the park until the army took over the

surveillance in 1886. In 1900 there were fewer than fifty animals left in Yellowstone. Today, after many years of careful management, the park accommodates several thousand animals, the only free-ranging bison herd in the USA. Another endangered species was the grizzly bear, which is abundant today but, like the wolf, suffered badly in the early days of the national park. The wolf met with the worst treatment. It was hunted recklessly for many decades in the USA because it killed sheep and cattle and was seen as a danger to people. As late as 1965 you could obtain a bounty of up to fifty dollars for a dead wolf, but the animals had already disappeared from Yellowstone by 1930. Not until March 1995, sixty-five years later, were fourteen Canadian wolves released into Yellowstone and at least nine pups born shortly afterward. The wolf is now reestablished.

On the great geyser plateaus it is as if a giant had danced on tiptoe with a palette and brush and spattered the landscape with the most improbable splashes of color. Specially adapted bacteria and algae create this kaleidoscope. Twenty miles (30km) west of Yellowstone Lake the Washburn expedition reached an area of natural springs that caused everything else to pale into insignificance—they were met by a 100-foot

You feel small when suddenly confronted by two grizzly bears in the forest.

The bison was close to extinction when it was saved under the protection of Yellowstone in 1872.

Yellowstone is the Earth's largest area of hot springs and Old Faithful is its most famous geyser.

(30m) high geyser. They quickly realized that it spurted regularly at hourly intervals. Dubbed Old Faithful by General Washburn, today it is probably the world's best-known geyser. Washburn's men gave other springs names that indicated something of their characteristics—the Beehive, the Castle, the Giant, the Fan, and the Cave. Some were called after gemstones that the shifting colors of the spring brought to mind—Topaz, Turquoise, Sapphire, Opal, and Emerald springs.

Farther north the Firehole River murmurs between one steaming vent and the next. There are thousands of springs, geysers, and bubbling holes in the ground in the national park—more than in the whole of the rest of the world. To the north lies Mammoth Hot Springs with its strange terrace formations of calcium carbonate and other compounds which have welled up from below ground and crystallized in the air.

The concept of a national park originated here in Yellowstone. Thanks to Washburn's expedition in 1870, the area became the world's first national park two years later. In 1978, as further proof of its outstanding character, it was among the first group of places to be registered by UNESCO as a World Heritage site.

YELLOWSTONE

REGISTERED: 1978.

COUNTRY: USA (Wyoming).

FORM OF CONSERVATION: National park, biosphere reserve.

CRITERIA: Geology, ecology, natural beauty, endangered species.

SIZE: 3,470 square miles (8,987sq km).

ALTITUDE: 5,600–11,350 feet (1,710–3,463m) above sea level.

LANDSCAPE: Forested area in the Rockies on a volcanic "hot spot." Last eruption 630,000 years ago. 6 major geyser plateaus, about 3,000 geysers, fumaroles, and hot springs. Yellowstone Lake, at 143 square miles (371sq km), is North America's largest mountain lake.

VEGETATION: 80% of the area is forest. Large number of skeletal trees from the 1988 fire. Seven species of coniferous trees and 1,100 vascular plants.

FAUNA: Grizzly and black bears, coyotes, and pumas. Wolves eradicated in the 1930s but reintroduced in 1995. 30,000 elks, 250 pronghorns, and 1,500 bison. Also bald eagles, peregrine falcons, and trumpeter swans.

CULTURAL HISTORY: 10,000-year-old Native American remains. 575 archaeological findings on 2% of the park area.

CONSERVATION VALUE: A geological archive of 55 million years of volcanic activity. The world's largest range of geothermal phenomena. Natural forest, grass plateaus, mountains, and water.

TOURISM: 3.1 million visitors per year (1999).

THREATS: Entered on the endangered list in 1995. Plans for quarrying, gas and oil extraction, and geoenergy production close to the park may destroy the grizzly bear's habitat.

—THE GIANTS OF THE COAST

The Roosevelt deer
(a form of the wapiti)
is a common sight on
the grasslands in
the redwood parks.

The coastal redwoods are
giants in the tree world.

Following pages: Jedediah
Smith Redwood State Park
is a hallowed cathedral
created by nature.

OUT OF THE MORNING MISTS RISES a mighty pillared hall of gray-brown fir trees on a vast scale. The coastal redwood tree, or American sequoia (*Sequoia sempervirens*), is the Earth's tallest tree, reaching 410 feet (125m) in height, 2,000 years in age, and taking 400 years to reach maturity. It is thanks to these trees that the redwood forest produces the greatest living weight per unit area of all ecosystems. On the slopes of the Sierra Nevada grows the giant tree, *Sequoiadendron giganteum*—not as tall as its relative but thicker, and up to 3,200 years old. It is the largest living being in terms of biomass per individual.

The national heritage sites of Redwood National and State Parks form a long green corridor comprising four reserves. We haul on our backpacks and step in among the columns of the Lady Bird Johnson Grove, or along the Tall Trees Trail in the national park to the south, or to Stout Grove in the Jedediah Smith Redwood State Park close to the Oregon boundary in the north—where you feel like Tom Thumb.

The last reserve is named after the trapper who was the first to reach California over the mountains from the east. Smith became fascinated by the redwood trees when he was trying to find the best route from the Rockies to the Pacific in 1828. At that time the Tolowa and Yurok Indians fished cutthroat trout and Chinook salmon in the rivers there, from their canoes of hollowed-out redwood trees. The redwood forest once covered 3,000 square miles (8,000sq km), almost the whole area of Yellowstone National Park. Today there is less than 5 percent, or 115-155 square miles (300–400sq km), left.

The coast of north California was of little value to the colonizing Englishmen and Spaniards until gold was discovered in 1850 at Gold Bluffs Beach, now part of the national park. When people failed to make their fortune from gold, the forests became a target. Until then nature had been able to withstand man. But once the railroad came in 1870, the bulldozer in 1920, and the timber lorries in 1940, the giant redwoods fell as never before and were exploited to provide timber for San Francisco's homes.

The coast of California is famous for its beauty. This includes the strip several hundred miles long, which comprises the redwood parks. Here the sea and the spacious, natural sandy beaches stretch away, ornamented with wild coastal cliffs. High Bluff Overlook and the little coast road above the precipice offer a site from which to obtain a magnificent view over the area. We meet a completely different world, fundamentally unlike the closed forest immediately above these sheer slopes.

A river flows into the ocean at Gold Bluffs Beach. The moisture from the Pacific is important to the survival of the redwood forest.

The redwood sorrel and ferns are typical decorative features of the forest carpet.

Where Prairie Creek flows out into the sea, in the reserve of the same name, we walk far into a deep canyon, which the stream has cut through the precipice. Its walls are vertical and hang over the diminutive human figure. Thanks to the constant trickle of moisture left behind by the mists, the precipitous walls of the narrow ravine are completely covered in ferns.

In the interior there is another world—Bald Hills. The bare, rolling mounds are covered with grass and this is one of the areas where you are most likely to see the Roosevelt deer grazing. It is yet another domain within the same heritage-rich site.

But there is nothing quite as impressive as the redwood tree, reaching closer to the sky than the Statue of Liberty. It produces straight timber that can resist both insects and decay, and in the forests it can withstand fires thanks to its thick nonresinous bark.

In the age of dinosaurs the climate was such that redwood forests covered large swathes of North America and the northern hemisphere. Later the climate became cooler and drier, but in some enclaves a favorable climate was preserved—as in the coastal tracts of northern California. Without the sea there would be no redwood forest.

REDWOOD

REGISTERED: 1980.

COUNTRY: USA (California).

FORM OF CONSERVATION: 1 national park, 3 state parks, biosphere reserve.

CRITERIA: Ecology, natural beauty.

SIZE: 290 square miles (752sq km).

ALTITUDE: 0–3,120 feet (950m) above sea level.

LANDSCAPE: Over 30 miles (48km) of rocky coastline with broad sandy beaches. Inland, hills of sedimentary bedrock with forests of tall coniferous trees.

VEGETATION: Coastal redwoods dominate. *Sequoia sempervirens*, the world's tallest trees, cover 61 square miles (158sq km). Coniferous trees such as Douglas firs, sitka pines, giant pines, and western hemlocks. Deciduous trees, such as broad-leafed maples and bay trees. 856 vascular plants recorded.

FAUNA: 75 mammals, such as Roosevelt deer or wapiti, black-tailed deer, bobcats, black bears, skunks, and otters. Rich marine wildlife with sea lions and cliff-dwelling seabirds. Endangered bird species, such as bald eagles and brown pelicans. 400 birds recorded.

CULTURAL HISTORY: Valuable prehistoric and historic sites dating back over 4,500 years.

CONSERVATION VALUE: Reserve with 42% of the remaining coastal redwood forest along the North American west coast.

TOURISM: 1.25 million visitors per year.

THE ROCKY MOUNTAINS
—CANADA'S BACKBONE

The peregrine falcon nests on the ledges of steep cliffs.

Takakkaw Falls in Yoho National Park are the highest falls in a World Heritage site at 833 feet (254m).

Following pages: Moraine Lake in Banff National Park is one of North America's most spectacular mountain lakes.

OUR CANADIAN CANOE shoots forward through the water with a gentle splash from the prow and the paddle. The still, opaline water turns the lake into a gemstone of polished turquoise. A solid, broad mountain of quartzite forms a massive backdrop, resting on scree slopes of weathered, fallen rock fragments. Its crest crowns Moraine Lake with a royal diadem of peaks rising up from one and the same fused body of stone.

More than any other mountain view, Moraine Lake is a picture postcard. This lake, with the Wenkchemna Peaks, is one of the most beautiful and majestic images of nature. The mountaineer and explorer Walter Wilcox, who first visited the shores of the lake in 1899, wrote that "No scene has given me an equal impression of inspiring solitude and rugged grandeur." Tourism had come with the railroad in 1883, but Moraine Lake and Wenkchemna Peaks—"the ten peaks"—first became famous after the Wilcox articles.

Many of the Rocky Mountain lakes conceal large holes in the land, hollowed out and filled with water from melted glaciers. Glacial lakes often change color to turquoise or emerald, owing to the finely ground particles of sand carried by the ice. A trail from Moraine Lake leads us to the Consolation lakes, where a larch forest surrounds several blue-green lakes. Other beautiful lakes are Lake Agnes and Lake Louise at Mount Victoria, Vermilion Lake near Banff, and Berg Lake on Mount Robson.

The Rocky Mountains are the backbone of North America. This is perhaps particularly true in Canada. The magnificent natural landscape has given rise to a group of national parks—Jasper, Banff, Yoho, and Kootenay—that lie adjacent to one another. Around this mighty core, like a kind of buffer, there is a series of provincial parks and wildlife reserves. The national parks and three of the provincial parks, which together cover an impressive 8,907 square miles (23,069sq km), were registered as a World Heritage site in 1984.

As we approach from Calgary in the east, mile upon mile of monotonously flat prairie leads us into an undulating landscape just over 3,200 feet (1,000m) high—the foothills of the Rocky Mountains. In several places we can see how the surface of the Earth has been squeezed so that the layers of sandstone and shale are vertical. Behind these fertile foothills the first mountains rise with dramatic effect. At Lac des Arcs we stand before a wall of gray limestone rock. The first mountains rise up more than

Competing male bighorn sheep may clash heads at 50–70mph (80–112kph).

The black-tailed prairie dog is not a dog but a rodent that lives in underground colonies.

It is easy to find vast, unspoiled areas in the Canadian Rockies.

Two wapitis wade in a river in Jasper National Park.

3,000 feet (900m) above the foothills in the east, and in part, lie on top of them. It is rare for layers with 400 million years' difference in age to lie so close together.

In the town of Banff we stand on the real backbone of the mountain chain itself—the high peaks exceeding 10,000 feet (3,000m) and the ridges of hard rock, such as quartzite, dolomite, and limestone. The massifs are often crowned with glaciers and the U-shaped valleys carved out by the glaciers are ornamented with lakes. The highest of all is Mount Robson at 12,972 feet (3,954m). Farther west, the topography settles down again into a softer, shale landscape, which folded into vertical strata when it met the pressure from the west. Here the valleys are V-shaped, created by the rivers rather than by the grinding of the glaciers.

As we walk beside a river in Jasper National Park, two stately wapitis suddenly appear before us, their well-developed antlers like the carved branches of a tree. In the background the river disappears behind the pine forest, which climbs on up the slopes. Such sights within the heart of the Rocky Mountains combine to create an image of the vigor and majesty of nature—a symbol of the real wilderness.

THE ROCKY MOUNTAINS

REGISTERED: 1984, extended 1990.

COUNTRY: Canada.

FORM OF CONSERVATION: 4 national parks, 3 provincial parks.

CRITERIA: Geology, ecology, natural beauty.

SIZE: 8,907 square miles (23,069sq km).

ALTITUDE: 3,400–12,970 feet (1,036–3,954m) above sea level.

LANDSCAPE: The area comprises the Rocky Mountains of Canada. Glaciers supply water for three river systems flowing into three different seas. Steep peaks. Canyons, waterfalls, and glacial lakes. World-famous fossils in the Burgess Shale.

VEGETATION: Dense forest, chiefly between 3,900–5,900 feet (1,200–1,800m). Douglas firs, silver firs, aspens, and poplars. Subalpine forest with lodgepole pine and Engelmann spruce. Alpine moors with low-growing willow and shrubs. Almost 1,000 species of vascular plants.

FAUNA: 56 mammal species. Predators such as grizzly and black bears, wolverines, wolves, lynxes, and pumas; ungulates such as moose, white-tailed deer, elks, bighorn sheep, and mountain goats. 280 bird species, such as golden eagles, ptarmigans, and three-toed woodpeckers.

CULTURAL HISTORY: Prehistoric sites at Vermilion Lake dating from 10,500BCE. Rock paintings in Kootenay. Trappers came during the 19th century, settlers with the railway in the 1880s.

CONSERVATION VALUE: Area of outstanding natural beauty with many threatened species. Examples of ongoing geological processes such as the formation of glaciers and gorges.

TOURISM: 8–10 million visitors per year.

WATERTON GLACIER

—MOUNTAINOUS FRONTIER LAND

A few mountain goats move across a steep slope. They like to climb cliff faces to reach the salt licks high up on narrow ledges.

Behind the river that flows into Upper Waterton Lake, the Rocky Mountains rise to 8,200 feet (2,500m) above sea level.

"**GOING TO THE SUN ROAD**"—so the route that crosses the magnificent American Glacier National Park is called. At Logans Pass we reach an altitude of 6,645 feet (2,026m) and all around us rise majestic peaks. Although they are not the highest of the Rocky Mountains, they seem imposing. The rock contains petrified sediment 1.5 billion years old, which the continental drift pushed up out of the sea when the Rocky Mountains were born 170 million years ago. The sediment became petrified but it never melted down, and so today geologists can still find sandstone showing unique marks of the folding process, as well as limestone containing fossils of some of the Earth's oldest life forms.

On the Canadian side of the area, Waterton Lakes was protected in 1895, first as a reserve to prevent oil prospecting in a virgin area and then later as a national park. In 1932 it was combined with the American Glacier National Park into what is now the world's only international peace park. The whole area is a spectacular wilderness, surrounded by developed and cultivated districts. In Waterton there is a small piece of natural prairie where bison have been introduced and the woodland is a haven for much of the larger wildlife. Two packs of wolves and around 200 grizzly bears—the most robust stock of grizzlies in the continental USA—range through the territory. The international peace park is both a wildlife paradise and a mountainous frontier land.

WATERTON GLACIER

REGISTERED: 1995.
COUNTRY: USA (Montana), Canada (Alberta).
FORM OF CONSERVATION: 2 national parks.
CRITERIA: Geology, ecology, natural beauty, threatened species.
SIZE: 1,765 square miles (4,575sq km).
ALTITUDE: 4,200–9,645 feet (1,280–2,939m) above sea level.

LANDSCAPE: Largely untouched mountainous region, rising sharply from the prairie. Some large lakes; several hundred small lakes. About 60 small glaciers.
VEGETATION: 13 square miles (33sq km) of untouched prairie Douglas firs and lodgepole pines; aspen woods at lower altitudes. Alpine moors with mountain avens

and poppies. 870 species of vascular plants.
FAUNA: Over 60 mammal species, such as wolves, pumas, black bears, and grizzlies. 240 bird species.
CULTURAL HISTORY: Archaeological sites up to 10,000 years old.
CONSERVATION VALUE: Outstanding landscape rich in wildlife.
TOURISM: 2 million visitors per year.

YOSEMITE

—THE GRANITE VALLEY

The granite cracks into large slabs as it weathers.

El Capitan, with its 3,604 feet (1,100m) drop, is the colossus of the valley and one of the world's highest vertical rock faces.

THE PEAKS THAT FRAME YOSEMITE are no ordinary mountain tops. Light-colored rocks shoot up straight as pillars into the blue sky, like giant buildings with flat façades, improbably clean and polished. But, although the granite is as smooth as a baby's head, the appearance of the mountains is severe because they are so steep. The tremendous elevation is even more imposing when we pick out the small silhouettes of trees on the top edge of the mountain. They lend it scale and give the illusion that the mountains are even bigger than they are.

The contrasts between harsh and gentle landscapes are extreme in Yosemite. "This valley is the only place that comes up to the brag about it, and exceeds it," wrote the nineteenth-century American essayist Ralph Waldo Emerson. In the valley there is space for alternating coniferous and deciduous woodland, pastoral flower meadows, and the Merced River, which runs through the valley like an artery. Here, too, there are roads, houses, and many people. The setting is something altogether different—a collection of "muscular," granite bodies competing for attention, adorned with some of the highest waterfalls in the world—the crescendo being Yosemite Falls at 2,425 feet (739m).

On the highly popular Half Dome we climb up a fixed iron ladder. Beneath our feet smooth slabs plunge straight down, giving us butterflies in our stomachs. The crest of this solid landmark runs out onto a plateau where we can cautiously approach the western precipice to peer 4,000 feet (1,220m) down into the valley bottom. The free drop is a full 2,000 feet (610m)—equivalent to two Eiffel Towers on top of each other.

Up here we can also see out over the Sierra Nevada, which John Muir, the Scottish-born naturalist, called "the Range of Light." He aroused many people's interest in this region at the end of the nineteenth century with his lyrical descriptions of the landscape. Gold prospectors had found their way here in 1849, but they came into immediate conflict with the Native Americans who were being driven out.

A decade later Frederick Olmsted, the inspiration behind Central Park in New York, suggested that the valley should belong to the American people, and, in 1864, President Lincoln signed the proposal that resulted in the establishment of the first nature conservation area. Twenty years later Yosemite was upgraded to a national park, covering a wide area of the wilderness as well as the valley.

The California Big Tree, or giant sequoia, is the Earth's largest living plant. It is found only on the western slopes of the Sierra Nevada.

The strenuous climb up the ladder on the Half Dome, with Cloud's Rest mountain, wreathed in smoke, in the background.

The Merced River runs through coniferous forest in Little Yosemite Valley.

Yosemite is the work of the Ice Age. Huge glaciers carved out this and several other deep valleys in the Sierra Nevada, and ground the mountainsides smooth. Today, there are just small residues of ice left in the highest massif. On lower levels there is coniferous forest, made up of many different species of trees. The national park also contains groups of giant sequoias, which need the earth to warm up so that their seeds can germinate. Every year lightning sparks off natural forest fires and the park administrators light controlled fires to keep the ecological cycle alive.

The national park has a good stock of black bears that are happy to forage for food where people camp. Incidents can occur when tourists are too inquisitive and the park rangers are sometimes forced to shoot refractory bears. To avoid this, bearproof steel boxes for storing supplies have been placed at official campsites along the trails.

Down in the Yosemite Valley conditions are more urban and crowded. Here there are regular bus routes, shopping centers, a police station, and so on. But up in the mountains the untouched and deserted landscape stretches away. This is another contrast in this amazingly beautiful and very popular national park.

YOSEMITE

REGISTERED: 1984.

COUNTRY: USA (California).

FORM OF CONSERVATION:
National park.

CRITERIA: Geology, ecology,
natural beauty.

SIZE: 1,190 square miles
(3,083sq km).

ALTITUDE: 2,201–13,115 feet
(671–3,998m) above sea level.

LANDSCAPE: Mountains, chiefly
comprising granite that has
been pushed upward. The tops
form domes, rounded peaks,
and high alpine massifs with
small glaciers. Larger glaciers
have sharpened the topography
and deepened the canyon-like
valleys. 300 lakes and
numerous high waterfalls.

VEGETATION: At lower levels
there is chaparral—dense
shrubby vegetation. The forests
contain 37 different species of
trees, such as tall, coniferous
trees like the Douglas fir
and the giant sequoia—
Sequoiadendron giganteum—
which reaches almost 35 feet
(10m) in diameter and 200 feet
(63m) in height. Alpine
meadows above the treeline.
1,300 species of vascular plants.

FAUNA: 74 species of mammals,
including pumas, red lynxes,
black bears, prairie wolves,
yellow-bellied marmots, and
black-tailed deer. 230 bird
species, among them golden
eagles, acorn woodpeckers,
and Steller's jays.

CULTURAL HISTORY: Inhabited by
Native Americans until the
mid-19th century. 1,000
archaeological sites have
been located.

CONSERVATION VALUE: Outstanding
scenic, mountainous area with
the character of a wilderness.
The national park contains
most of the native species
of the Sierra Nevada.

TOURISM: 4 million visitors
per year.

GRAND CANYON
—A WINDOW ON THE UNDERWORLD

The beaver-tail cactus flowers in the spring.

Havasu Canyon, where the river is colored blue-green by the limestone of its springs, is one of the biggest lateral ravines.

Following pages: Sunset over Grand Canyon, seen here from Hopi Point on the southern edge, is a blaze of color.

THE ROAD ACROSS THE COCNINO PLATEAU IS FLANKED BY PINE FORESTS. After some miles the trees suddenly thin out and the air beyond seems to change in the same way that it does just before you reach the sea. We arrive at Mather Point, and when we see Grand Canyon for the first time, we cannot believe our eyes. We look out over a chaotic world of ravines, ravines, and more ravines—and between them are freestanding mountains, some as slim as arrows, others as broad as fortresses. The edge of the chasm on the other side is a distant, shimmering contour. There is both a liberating span and a terrifying depth to the view—and below lies an enclosed landscape that instantly captures our attention.

This peerless natural scenery is so extraordinary that we fumble for points of reference to explain what we can see. In order to explore this canyon we have to go mountaineering in reverse—first down, and then back up. From Mather Point an impressive portion of the ravine landscape is revealed, but it is still impossible to comprehend the whole. With the many nooks and crannies in the ravines, and its forgotten corners and inaccessible peaks, Grand Canyon is a world all of its own.

The Colorado River took just four million years to cut out this window to the inside of the Earth, a short time in geological terms. The river encountered layer after layer of different kinds of rock. The youngest was on top, a 250-million-year-old limestone, and in the deepest parts almost two-billion-year-old primary rock have been uncovered. The tributaries developed lateral ravines, which have turned Grand Canyon into a finely branched nervous system. A number of volcanic eruptions occurred in the western section several million years ago. A stream of lava ran down into the bottom of the gorge and dammed up an enormous lake, but in the end the pressure of the water smashed the barrier and only huge boulders were left behind. After this cataclysm the notorious Lava Falls—the most dangerous falls of all—came into being,

Today, the Colorado River runs 5,000 feet (1,500m) below the plateaus and the rock walls form a giant stairway, which is also an open textbook of geology. Where the strata consist of hard rock, sheer precipices have formed, but where the rock is softer the slopes are tamer. As we tramp down to the depths we are walking far back into the history of the Earth. The path twists first through layers of limestone, then down through shale followed by sandstone, and again through the same sequence, until

Agaves grow in the desert-like environment on the ledges lower down the ravine.

Tourists on muleback pass by the green oasis of Indian Garden on their way down to the Colorado River.

Geological erosion fills the Colorado River with brownish-red mud, which has given the river its Spanish name.

we finally reach granites and gneiss in the innermost cleft of primary rock. The walk is also a journey from one climate to another. On the high plateaus, 6,500-feet plus (2,000m), the climate is not unlike that of northern Europe. On the northern side, which is higher than the south, there is heavy snow in winter. There, coniferous forest grows, with aspen and stands of western yellow pine and oak. In contrast, the depths of the canyon are carpeted with a desert-like bush vegetation of agaves and cactuses.

The first Native Americans reached Grand Canyon 11,000 years ago. Much later the mysterious Anasazi people emerged, but they abandoned the canyon in the thirteenth century, for reasons unknown. During the fifteenth century the forefathers of the present-day Hualapai and Huvasupai peoples arrived, two tribes who now have their own reservation in the western reaches of Grand Canyon. Road and air traffic is considerable and air pollution from Los Angeles, 400 miles (650km) to the west, sometimes lays a cap of smog over the canyon. On the surrounding plateaus there are small tourist centers with modern facilities. Down at the bottom a savage and untamed landscape still greets us—the most magnificent natural scenery you can imagine.

GRAND CANYON

REGISTERED: 1979.

COUNTRY: USA (Arizona).

FORM OF CONSERVATION:
National park.

CRITERIA: Geology, ecology,
natural beauty, threatened
species.

SIZE: 1,900 square miles
(4,930sq km).

ALTITUDE: 1,700–9,152 feet
(518–2,793m) above sea level.

LANDSCAPE: Gigantic canyon, 45
miles (72km) long and 1 mile
(1.6km) deep. Varies in breadth
from a half to 20 miles
(0.5–30km). Quantities of
residual rock stand isolated in
the canyon, which has been dug
out by the Colorado River.

VEGETATION: Forests chiefly of
conifers, aspen, and maple up
on the plateaus. Down in the
canyon, desert vegetation with
cactuses. 1,500 species of
vascular plants.

FAUNA: 76 mammals, including
prairie wolves, pumas,
bobcats, and several species
of cloven-hoofed animals.
300 bird species, including the
bald-eagle. 50 different types of
reptiles and amphibians.

CULTURAL HISTORY: Large number of
sites and ruins from the Anasazi
people. Hualapai and Havasupai
tribes still living on reservations
outside the national park.

CONSERVATION VALUE: The world's
biggest canyon and an
outstanding monumental
landscape.

TOURISM: 5 million visitors
per year.

EVERGLADES

—RIVER OF GRASS

An unusually flamboyant
grasshopper pauses for a
moment in Taylor Slough.

From the Anhinga Trail
there is a sweeping view
over the "river of grass,"
where alligators lurk
in the water.

FROM PA-HAY-OKEE, one of the excursion destinations in the Everglades National Park, a panoramic view unfolds—grass as far as the eye can see. The indigenous population, Native Americans of the Miccosukee and Seminole tribes, gave their land the name of Pa-hay-okee, which encapsulates exactly what it is—a "river of grass."

"There are no other Everglades in the world," wrote the author Marjory Stoneman Douglas in 1947, the same year that President Harry S. Truman inaugurated the area as a national park. In her book, *The Everglades: River of Grass*, she described with respect and affection this remarkable phenomenon in southern Florida, which is not actually a river in the true sense of the word, but a shallow 6-inch (15cm) deep watercourse running through an 8-mile (12.8km) wide sea of 10-foot (3m) high sawgrass. The Everglades was a "vast glittering openness, wider than the enormous visible round of the horizon."

From the Royal Palms Visitor Center a system of wooden bridges, known as the Anhinga Trail, runs above the water and through the high grass. Fish move around the stones; alligators lie in wait for freshwater turtles, which swim with just their nostrils above water; herons stand motionless, poised to ambush the fish. Nearby, smoke rises over the treetops as the park administrators burn dry grass to promote new growth.

During a boat trip from Flamingo in the bird-rich wetlands of Whitewater Bay, along the Buttonwood Canal, the mangrove thickets close tightly around us, with their tangle of oxygen-absorbing roots. They protect against erosion and provide breeding grounds for a multiplicity of marine species. Wherever there is a stretch of beach, crocodiles and alligators take their rest.

More than 300 species of bird nest in these rich biotopes. Plants, animals, and birds of land and water have adapted to one another in the course of evolution—and to the seasonal climate with its hot, dry winters and wet, mosquito-ridden summers. Some rare animal species have been given special protection by the authorities—for example alligators, manatees, the Florida puma, and herons. Six species of animal are threatened with extinction, sixteen are on the list of vulnerable species. Since the 1930s the nesting colonies of wading birds have diminished from 265,000 to 18,500. Numbers of the endangered wood stork have dropped from 6,000 in the 1960s to 500 today. The present crocodile population amounts to no more than 400 animals.

A green heron waits
patiently for a catch.

A cypress grove gives some
shade, on the road to
Mahogany Hammock.

Florida's alligators are
extremely partial to these
freshwater turtles.

A technicolor sunset
provides a spectacular
backdrop for a barn owl.

Over the ages Lake Okeechobee has broken its banks during the rainy season, with the result that water has flooded southward over the grasslands to the coast. As early as 1916 the last stretch was dug of the 200 miles (322km) of canals, which had taken thirty years to construct. The vast, unprofitable, waterlogged, mosquito-producing grassland was to be drained for the benefit of a healthy and profitable agriculture.

The total ecosystem comprises more than half of southern Florida. Exploitation of any part of it also affects the balance within the World Heritage site. In spite of ten protective buffer zones around the national park, the nature conservation arrangements barely cover half of this ecosystem. Over the last several decades the park authorities have tried to restore the Everglades' natural water cycles—a difficult and costly project.

When dusk has fallen something almost miraculous appears in the glow of our car headlights—a Florida puma! This is a sight one no longer expects to see. It is thought that there are just thirty animals left. A couple of nimble leaps and the puma has crossed the road and disappeared into the trees. To see this endangered species about 100 feet (30m) away, even for a few fleeting moments, is a gift indeed.

EVERGLADES

REGISTERED: 1979.

COUNTRY: USA (Florida).

FORM OF CONSERVATION: National park, biosphere reserve.

CRITERIA: Geology, ecology, endangered species.

SIZE: 2,340 square miles (6,067sq km).

ALTITUDE: 0–6 feet (0–2m) above sea level.

LANDSCAPE: Flat lowland on limestone, which prevents the surface water from draining. Subtropical marine area.

VEGETATION: Dry wooded islands; species of mango, sawgrass, willow and cypress. Everglades' flora with 950 vascular plants is unique in the USA because of the high proportion of endemic and Caribbean species.

FAUNA: 800 species of land and water vertebrates, including 25 native mammals. Approximately 30 Florida pumas and 1,200 manatees. Over 400 bird species; 275 fish species; 60 reptile and amphibian species.

CULTURAL HISTORY: 20 archaeological sites; prehistoric Miccosukee relics.

CONSERVATION VALUE: North America's only subtropical national park. 14 endangered species and the largest number of nesting tropical wading birds on the continent.

TOURISM: 1.2 million visitors per year.

THREATS: Added to endangered list in 1993. Increasing population pressure. Canals affecting water flow and biological cycles. Foreign species driving out native ones.

SOUTH AMERICA

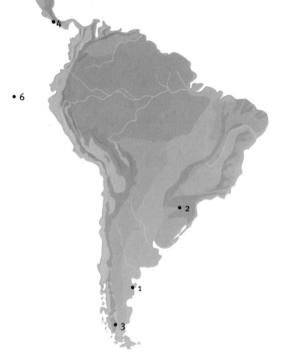

With South America we include Central America and the Caribbean islands. The backbone of this continent is the Andes, the Earth's longest mountain chain. In the north of the continent lies the Earth's largest rainforest—the Amazon; south of the range are the grassy plains of the pampas, and farther south again, the dry, desert tableland of Patagonia. The natural heritage of South America has often been selected for its ecological value and threatened species, but several of the World Heritage sites also comprise coastal stretches, marine environments, and islands that are highly valued precisely because of their rich animal life. We describe sites based on our walking tours, from the mountains of Los Glaciares in the south to the jungles of the Maya in the north, including the volcanic Galápagos islands, the dry forests of Guanacaste, the teeming bays along the Atlantic coast, and the Earth's most extensive system of waterfalls on the Brazil–Argentina border.

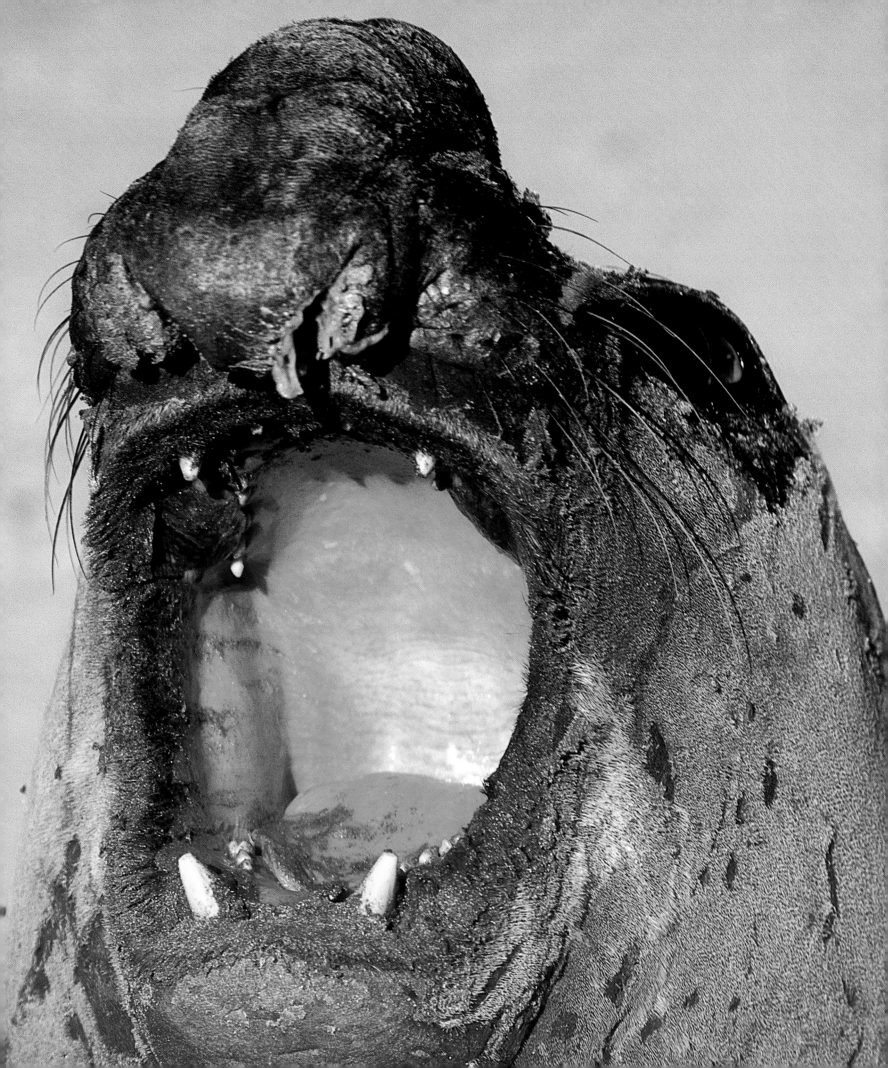

—EMPTY DESERT, TEEMING SEA

40,000 pairs of Magellanic penguins live along the coast of the Valdés Peninsula.

The coast north of Punta Delgada shelters several colonies of sea lions and elephant seals.

THE ROAD TO THE VALDÉS PENINSULA cuts in a straight line through the seemingly endless Patagonian landscape. Patagonia begins in the north where the grassy plains of the pampas end, and extends right down to Tierra del Fuego. The gently rolling plain is monotonous but at the same time fascinating and irresistible in its breadth and space. Patagonia, of which Valdés is a part, is a desert and a steppe: waterless, windswept, vast and sun-scorched—sparsely populated with bushes that have adopted rounded contours to withstand the wide open forces of nature. There is an Argentinian saying: "If you want to see Patagonia you just have to sit still long enough and it will blow past you."

An eleven-hour expedition in dire conditions gave Charles Darwin more of an insight into Patagonia than most people. Yet he was fascinated and asked himself: "Why then have these arid wastes taken so firm possession of my mind? … I can scarcely analyse these feelings, but it must be partly owing to the free scope given to the imagination." Patagonia engenders both love-hate and respect.

Not far from the cracked surface of Salinas Grande's salt lake we have the good fortune to glimpse in the distance a timid mara from the bush steppes, a large rodent with long hind legs and short ears. Reminding one of a small kangaroo, it is also called the pampas hare and belongs to the guinea pig family. We also encounter the Patagonian gray fox, the armadillo, the sand grouse, and the elegant crested tinamou. One large mammal, which we cannot miss, is the guanaco—the wild Andean llama—which is one of the continent's four members of the family *Camelidae*.

We often see flocks of guanacos with the mountain rhea or "ñandu"—the smaller of two species of ostrich-like birds, originally named *Rhea darwini* after the man who discovered it. This ecological symbiosis corresponds to that seen between the ostriches and ungulates in Africa, which frequently graze together to take mutual advantage of the different skills they possess in detecting predators at a distance.

During his visit to the pampas in 1834 Darwin heard tell of a small species of rhea. Subsequently, farther south down the coast, the ship's artist shot one, which the crew prepared and ate. Replete with this dinner Darwin suddenly recollected the rumor of the smaller species. Unfortunately, by then the bird had already been consumed, but he took its bones and skin back to England, where the zoologist John Gould discovered

that it was indeed a new species and named it after Darwin. However, the lesser rhea was later given a different scientific name, *Pterocnemia pennata*.

In sharp contrast to the barren desert plateau found on land, a highly diverse marine life flourishes along the coast, thanks to the Falkland Current, cold and rich in plankton, which sweeps up from the south. The marine environs of the Valdés Peninsula are particularly favored because they are partly sheltered by several large bays whose calm, clear waters attract seabirds, sea lions, great whales, and dolphins.

The Golfo San José is a bay curving into the peninsula from the north, while the Golfo Nuevo curves in from the south. This creates the narrow "wasp waist" of the Ameghino Isthmus, binding Valdés to the mainland like a label to a lapel. Seven nature reserves, including these two bays, have been set up on Valdés by the farsighted provincial government of Chubut, which understood early on—as far back as the mid-1970s it was anticipating the future value of ecotourism—that its nature tourists would generate a longer-term income than hunters. Together the seven nature reserves constitute the UN World Heritage site of the Valdés Peninsula.

In the Golfo San José lies the interesting Isla de los Pájaros (Bird Island) roughly half a mile (1km) out at low tide. Flamingos shimmer like a distant pink ribbon north of the island, while at Punta Norte sea lions and southern elephant seals disport themselves in large herds of quivering blubber. We follow the eastern coast along the Caleta Valdés, a strange lagoon created by a long sandbar running parallel with the coast for 3 miles (5km). In several places we meet Magellanic penguins, a species that once suffered exploitation for its oil, but which has now recovered—today there are almost 40,000 pairs on the Valdés Peninsula. We spend the night at the lighthouses of Punta Delgada in the southeast and before sunrise we set off down the steep slope to the beach. As the sun rises over the Atlantic horizon our only company is a few still drowsy elephant seals.

Golfo Nuevo is surrounded by steep sandy-colored cliffs that are striped with layers of sediment, which accrued during the time when they were at the bottom of the sea. The strata of the cliffs form a flipchart of past epochs in geological history and are a paradise for fossil-hunters. Places like this gave Darwin a better understanding of the time spans covered by his theory of evolution.

A dolphin photographed
in a mid-air arc in the
Golfo Nuevo.

Sturdy sheep on the
Patagonian plain.

The mountain rhea—
South America's ostrich—
is often found in the
company of guanacos.

Above the cliffs sea lions congregate with rock shags, while in the sea below the gleaming black fin of a killer whale slices the surface. Like the threatened southern "right" whale, it comes here to breed in the southern hemisphere's springtime. Valdés is known for the killer whale's special method of hunting. It "creeps" closer and closer to the beach where sea lions are swimming or resting. Then, it charges into the shallow water and often manages to sink its teeth into an unsuspecting pup.

The "right" whale was named thus by whalers a long time ago, because it was easy prey and therefore the "right" species to hunt. It moves slowly because of its large head, which has evolved to accommodate the fringes of keratin that hang from its upper jaw and act as a strainer with which to catch shellfish and plankton.

By boat we encounter a large pod of small whales—dolphins—bubbling over with *joie de vivre* and leaping up from the sea in elegant arcs as they hunt and play in groups. They present an incredible spectacle when they pop up like this, several hundred at a time. There are not many places in the world that can offer encounters with whales such as these in the sea around the Valdés Peninsula.

VALDÉS PENINSULA

REGISTERED: 1999.

COUNTRY: Argentina.

FORM OF CONSERVATION: 7 nature reserves.

CRITERIA: Threatened species.

SIZE: 1,390 square miles (3,600sq km).

ALTITUDE: 115 feet–330 feet (35–100m) above sea level.

LANDSCAPE: Peninsula with narrow neck to mainland. Dry, fairly flat steppe with saltwater pools. 40 miles (65km) of coast.

VEGETATION: Desert-like steppe with *Stipa* and *Poa* grass.

130 species of plant from 41 families, 38 of which are endemic to Argentina.

FAUNA: Southern "right" whales, killer whales, and dolphins. The southern sea lion and southern elephant seal have major colonies along the beaches. Guanacos, Argentinian gray foxes, armadillos, and timid maras. 181 bird species, of which 66 are migratory. Five colonies of Magellanic penguins, totaling at least 40,000 pairs. Rheas or ñandus, kelp gulls, two species of cormorant, migratory shorebirds.

CULTURAL HISTORY: Valdés was discovered in 1779 by the Spaniards who built a fort at La Candelaria.

CONSERVATION VALUE: Unique breeding ground for marine mammals. Half the world's southern "right" whales come here every year.

TOURISM: 140,000 tourists per year, of whom 80% are Argentinian.

IGUAÇÚ/IGUAZÚ

—WHERE CLOUDS ARE BORN

Visitors shrouded in
mists from the falls.

The vapor from Iguaçú Falls
encourages plants known
as epiphytes to grow
on the trees.

IT IS AS IF NATURE HAD SEARCHED extra hard before she chose the site of Foz do Iguaçú in the matted South American jungle. Before we saw it we had been unable to imagine how a waterfall could spread out so wide. In contrast to all other falls and cataracts in the world, we need to travel miles around this most spectacular water show.

We do not want to see just limited fragments of this World Heritage site, we would really like to experience it as a whole—as it bursts forth from the rainforest, first to surround, and then to cast itself down the Devil's Throat, or Garganta del Diablo, with a thundering cacophony of sound.

The Iguaçú River rises quite close to the south coast of Brazil, in the Serra do Mar Mountains, which reach no more than about 4,265 feet (1300m) above sea level, and then it meanders just over 50 miles (80km) inland. There, the river is joined by a large number of tributaries, which add volume and power, and then it suddenly bends at a right angle in a shape resembling an elbow. Immediately after that it flows over the cliffs on both sides of the 250-foot (76m) deep canyon, which the river has eroded in the basalt foundation. The whole network rests on a lava plateau that was pushed up to the surface of the Earth, more than 135 million years ago. On the inside of the river bend, most of the water cascades into the innermost part of the gorge. This occurs across a long line of falls, which are all more or less separate from each other—the main ones being the Union, Floriano, Rivadavia, and Belgrano falls.

Around the outside of these central falls, the river spreads over a wide area of the underlying plateau and reaches the main bed and the gorge after a circuitous move that creates a large "lake," which forms the outer part of the "elbow." When the water reaches the gorge again it is along a front a couple of miles wide on the southern, Argentinian side of the river, where it is called the Iguazú. The water finds it way to the edge between San Martin Island and many other wooded islands, which break up the falling water into the San Martin Falls and a series of greater and smaller waterfalls.

The Iguaçú River forms the border between Brazil and Argentina. Three quarters of the almost 2-mile (3km) wide falls are on the Argentinian side. The islands and the mainland close to the falls are resplendent with dark green rainforest that is sprayed continually with a cloud of fine water droplets, which benefits the vegetation.

Luxuriant, deep green rainforest surrounds the gorge at Iguaçú.

The curtain of the waterfall extends almost 2 miles (3km) around the Devil's Throat.

Moisture is also apparent in the variety of species we find everywhere, in the different layers of vegetation in the rainforest and the lush meadows beside the falls. Trees 100-foot (30m) high form the canopy, while the subvegetation reveals ferns, pepper bushes, legumes, myrtle, and bamboo. Up tree trunks and along branches ramble bromeliad rosettes, *Compositae* genera, tree ferns, begonias, and around sixty types of orchid. Botanists have counted some 2,000 plant species in the World Heritage site that surrounds the falls, while zoologists have observed more than 400 bird species and almost seventy mammals. The myriad butterflies are an experience in themselves.

The first European to see the falls was the Spanish explorer Alvar Nuñes in 1541, who was also known as Cabeza de Vaca—"cowhead"! The indigenous people he met, the Tupí-Guaraní, had lived in the rainforest for thousands of years. They called the waterfall "the place where the clouds are born" and "Iguaçú," which means "the great water." When Jesuit monks arrived here at the beginning of the seventeenth century they used Iguaçú Falls, which the Tupí-Guaraní regarded as holy place, as a base from which to speak of higher powers.

IGUAÇÚ/IGUAZÚ

REGISTERED: 1984.

COUNTRY: Brazil–Argentina.

FORM OF CONSERVATION: 2 national parks, 1 nature reserve.

CRITERIA: Natural beauty, threatened species.

SIZE: 212 square miles (550sq km).

ALTITUDE: 490–555 feet (150–170m) above sea level.

LANDSCAPE: Almost 2-mile (3km) wide waterfall around a gorge, of which half a mile is in Brazil. Islands and cliffs divide the falls into 150–270 smaller ones— depending on the volume of water. The average drop is 235 feet (72m) and the river tumbles down into a narrow gorge cut into the underlying basalt rock.

VEGETATION: Falls are surrounded by the unusual, subtropical rainforest of Paraná, with a wealth of lianas, epiphytes, and trees almost 100 feet (30m) tall. 3 variants distinguished—the islands variant is dependent on constant moisture. 2,000 species of flowering plants, including 60 orchids.

FAUNA: Rich animal life with 68 different mammals, such as giant otters, River Plate otters, jaguars, and ocelots. 422 bird species. 38 reptiles, including rattlesnakes and caymans.

CULTURAL HISTORY: The first inhabitants were the Kaingang, who were driven out by the Tupí-Guaraní. At least 2 sites of archaeological interest exist.

CONSERVATION VALUE: Magnificent waterfall and rare rainforest; large number of threatened species, particularly birds.

TOURISM: 500,000 visitors per year.

THREATS: The Brazilian part was put on the threatened list in 1999 because of an illegally opened road, increased helicopter traffic, and proposals for a new dam upstream of the Iguaçú River.

LOS GLACIARES

—ICE AND GRANITE

The guanaco is one of South America's four members of the *Camelidae* family.

The cool blue Perito Moreno Glacier is one of the most beautiful in the world.

Following pages: The first rays of the sun strike Cerro Torre, Fitz Roy, and the peaks around them, behind the village of Chaltén.

GENTLY THE CURTAIN OF THE NIGHT RISES and the magnificent south Argentinian mountain landscape takes shape to greet a new day. Its towers and pinnacles rise above the surrounding hills and plateaus. There is Cerro Torre, at 10,262 feet (3,128m) the most gangling of them, loyally supported by 9,510-foot (2,900m) high Torre Egger and Cerro Standhardt at 9,185 feet (2,800m). Farther to the right we have the captain himself, Fitz Roy, which at 11,285 feet (3,441m) stands higher and is more solid than these two, flanked in turn by his steadfast protectors, Aguja Saint Exupéry at 8,790 feet (2,680m), Poincenot at 10,049 feet (3,063m), and Mermoz at an altitude of 11,289 feet (3,441m). Soon the peaks glow in the morning sun. As the sun rises higher the granite loses its rosy hue and pales slowly to a leaden gray. The path here winds steeply through a pastoral mountain landscape, its slopes swathed in a dark green girdle of small-leaved, southern beech forest. It feels unreal—like walking in a steep olive grove in Italy at 4,000 feet (1,220m)—surrounded by bare hills and cold glaciers in the west and treeless Patagonian tableland in the east.

Soon we shall see Fitz Roy's impenetrable hood of cloud. The Fuego people believed that this mountain was a volcano because there was always "smoke" around its top. After a three-hour wait we see how the cloud disperses and exposes the impressive massif, its pinnacles chiseled by glaciers, as naturally castellated architecture of the finest kind. And the light! The back-lighting, when the sun goes down behind the Andes in the west, glorifies the lingering veils of cloud, while the peaks themselves have become blue-black silhouettes protruding from the decorative trimming.

"But we viewed in these grand mountains with regret, for we were obliged to imagine about their form and nature, instead of standing, as we had hoped, on their crest, and looking down on the plain below." These were Charles Darwin's words after Captain Robert Fitzroy's expedition into the interior. Twenty-five men in three whaleboats left the frigate *Beagle* in January 1834 and worked their way up the Santa Cruz River for three weeks. The river originates from Lago Argentino, which drains the glaciers around the Fitz Roy massif. These areas of mountains and glaciers today make up the World Heritage site of Los Glaciares. The disappointed Fitzroy did not reach these heights but at least he had a magnificent mountain peak named after him.

Fitz Roy, encircled by Aguja Saint Exupéry, Poincenot, and Mermoz.

A crested caracara surveys its surroundings.

Cerro Torre flanked by Torre Egger and Cerro Standhardt.

A closer look at Perito Moreno Glacier.

Los Glaciares National Park is fascinating in its contrasts. In the southern part we fasten crampons to our boots and stride out across the Perito Moreno Glacier. The enormous ice mass unfurls its broad tongue halfway across the channel to the Magellan Peninsula, where we watch the movements and rumbling divisions of the high ice front at close quarters. The glacier arches upward, backward, and in over the south Andean cordillera to become one with the Earth's biggest permanent snow and ice field outside Antarctica. Channels beginning at different tongues of the glacier form arms of Lago Argentino. Not far from here we travel by boat up the channel of the Brazo Norte to the Upsala Glacier. The ice masses drain into these lake-like branches that conduct the meltwater to Lago Argentino, on along the Santa Cruz River, and out to the Atlantic Ocean.

What makes Los Glaciares such an extraordinary experience is the forest—a unique deciduous forest with three closely related southern species of beech growing right up close to the glacier. In the fall the forest is a warm reddish-yellow color, as it stretches out toward the cold, everlasting, blue-white ice to offer a contrast of a kind rarely seen.

LOS GLACIARES

REGISTERED: 1981.

COUNTRY: Argentina.

FORM OF CONSERVATION: National park.

CRITERIA: Ecology, natural beauty.

SIZE: 1,721 square miles (4,459sq km).

ALTITUDE: 655–11,070 feet (200–3,375m) above sea level.

LANDSCAPE: System of glaciers wedged in between sharp peaks in the cordillera of the southern Andes. The biggest are the Upsala Glacier, with 230 square miles (595sq km), and the Viedma, with 222 square miles (575sq km). With 45 other glaciers they form the Patagonian ice mass of 5,405 square miles (14,000sq km).

VEGETATION: The dry Patagonian tableland in the east is dominated by *Festuca*, *Stipa*, and *Poa* grasses. Unique forest of three southern beech species, which grows right up close to the glaciers.

FAUNA: Guanacos and Argentine gray foxes. Isolated population of southern Andean huemuls, lesser rheas, Andean condors, torrent ducks, several species of caracara. 100 bird species.

CULTURAL HISTORY: Remains of prehistoric people who hunted guanacos; Tehuelche people more or less eradicated by Europeans.

CONSERVATION VALUE: Magnificent mountain and glacier landscape with an important role in the hydrology of the region. Small number of threatened species.

TOURISM: 78,000 tourists per year, mostly Argentinians.

GUANACASTE

—RESCUED DRY FOREST

The keel-billed toucan lives on mainly fruit and insects in the lowland jungle.

The genuine, tropical dry forest is more endangered than the rainforest. In Central America only two percent of it remains.

THE TANGLED PRIMARY FOREST on the Cacáo volcano is dense; we get caught up in creepers—and scratch ourselves on the sharp thorns, which are just one of the jungle's arsenal of defensive weapons. We push on toward its twin volcano of Orosí, close by. The steep cone of Orosí rises up from a bed of primeval mountain rainforest. The vegetation along the invisible paths is ever more stunted and hung with lichens. Trunks and branches are festooned with hanging lichens, mosses, and bromeliad rosettes. Farther up the slopes of the crater, airy, primeval tree ferns are increasingly common.

For at least eleven months of the year the volcanoes of Cacáo and Orosí are shrouded in persistent veils of cloud. The droplets of moisture from the mists condense on the leaves in the stunted forest, trickle down the slopes and form streams, which run even in the dry season. On this day the cloud forest, despite its name, is completely free of cloud, allowing us a magnificent view from the rim of the crater down over the dry forest and savanna of Santa Rosa. When the sun burns down, life on the dry lowland is sustained by the moisture from the mountain forests on Cacáo and Orosí.

The interplay between the ecosystems at the different altitudes is necessary not only for the plants, but also for the mammals and insects. In addition to fostering moisture, during the hot months from December to April the mountain forest serves as a refuge for many dry forest species, particularly moths. When the rains come in May these species go back down to Santa Rosa to produce new generations.

The science guru of Guanacaste is Professor Daniel Janzen from the University of Pennsylvania. For several decades now he has been collecting, studying, and describing the interaction between the different biotopes and their flora and fauna. Without Janzen's research endeavors Guanacaste would not be a World Heritage site today. Here we find a whole precious ecological spectrum of Central American natural environments, which have all but disappeared elsewhere. The World Heritage site comprises everything from the coastal waters and semiwet forests of Naranjo Beach on the Pacific to Santa Rosa's eternally green dry forest of oak and guanapinol, and the profusion of moisture-retaining vegetation that is tangled around the volcanic cones.

The 230 square miles (600sq km) of neotropical dry forest is probably the biggest protected area of this type of habitat anywhere. This biotope is far more endangered

than the rainforest. For one thing it was less extensive originally, and for another it was easier to chop down and cultivate. Santa Rosa's sparsely wooded savannas are dry forest that has been turned into grazing for livestock. It was the Spanish conquistadors who, at the end of the sixteenth century, laid the foundations for a gigantic ranch in Santa Rosa of some 270 square miles (700sq km). Today, slightly smaller, the area is being left for the original dry forest species to recolonize, but the process is also being helped by planting.

Apart from a diversity of landscapes, this World Heritage site also hosts an impressive array of animals. There are 20,000 species of beetles, 5,000 butterflies, and 500 birds. Howler monkeys, cats, bats, a total of 150 species of mammals, all share their living space in Guanacaste with 100 or so species of snakes, lizards, and amphibians.

Around midnight we are sitting by the Pacific Ocean as the moon rises in the star-strewn, natural planetarium above us. A mighty leatherback turtle appears slowly at the water's edge, before it lumbers laboriously up the beach to lay its eggs. Every winter a quarter of a million sea turtles set out on the same adventure, a scene reminiscent of a bygone age when evolution could continue undisturbed by humankind.

GUANACASTE

REGISTERED: 1999.

COUNTRY: Costa Rica.

FORM OF CONSERVATION: 3 national parks, 1 wildlife reserve.

CRITERIA: Ecology, threatened species.

SIZE: 505 square miles (1,310sq km), of which 166 square miles (430sq km) is marine environment.

ALTITUDE: 6,285 feet (1,916m) above sea level.

LANDSCAPE: Sea, beach, coastal cliffs, lowland, mountain slopes, and 3 active volcanoes. Extends from the Pacific down to the lowland on the Atlantic side.

VEGETATION: Mangrove thickets on the coast in the west, savanna and tropical dry forest on the lowland, mountain rainforest on the volcanoes, and lowland rainforest on the eastern side of the mountains. Lowland forest with deciduous trees, evergreen forests, oak forest, and savanna.

FAUNA: Mammals such as howler and capuchin monkeys, tapirs, peccaries, anteaters, and jaguars. More than 500 bird species. 250,000 turtles from 4 species. 20,000 beetle species; 13,000 species of hymenopterans, such as bees and wasps.

CULTURAL HISTORY: Santa Rosa, one of the first cattle ranches in Central America, established 1580–1600. Monument to the battle at Santa Rosa in 1856, and the country's independence in 1956–7.

CONSERVATION VALUE: Central America's biggest remaining area of neotropical dry forest. Many threatened species.

TOURISM: 64,000 visitors per year—half of them from other countries.

TIKAL

—THE JUNGLE OF MAYAN TEMPLES

A white-nosed coati pauses on the steps of the Temple of the Two-Headed Serpent.

The moon passes over the Temple of the Great Jaguar, which is 140 feet (42m) high.

Following pages: Above the carpet of the rainforest rise mysterious pyramids.

THE NIGHT IS PITCH BLACK AS WE CLIMB the 200 feet (60m) to the top of the pyramid of the Two-Headed Serpent, the highest temple in the Mayan city of Tikal in the jungles of northern Guatemala. A toucan breaks the silence as it clears its throat, using its strange bill as an echo chamber. At the same moment dawn comes creeping in and slowly reveals a carpet of green that spreads out wide below us, closely woven together with leaves, twigs, vines, and lianas. From this photosynthetic cloth rise strange, isolated, limestone pyramids created by man.

The forest around the temples awakes. Things are shrouded in mist, which in our imaginations represents smoke lingering from the fires once lit by the Maya in the city. The mysterious dawn and the glimpse of the pyramids carry us back more than a thousand years to the late ninth century CE: Tikal and the Mayan culture in Central America are at their height. Thousands of people are walking along the 80-foot (25m) wide avenues toward the market places in the heart of the city. The 90,000 inhabitants live in the surrounding area, where 3,000 buildings are scattered over hundreds of square miles.

The rainforest supplies the Maya with food and useful materials. From the bedrock they carve the limestone blocks for their buildings. Bread, vegetables, and edible roots are their staple food. They grind the protein-rich fruits of the breadnut tree, or *ramón*, to make flour, which they form into tortillas, bake as chestnut-scented bread, or make into soup. Deer, iguanas, and ocellated turkeys provide meat. Various palm trees yield roofing materials, fiber for clothes and mats, oil, and edible flowers. The Maya obtain skins from mammals, such as monkeys and big cats, and fish from the lakes nearby.

In the rainforest there grows the cordoncillo shrub, which contains an antidote to snakebite; the cinchona tree, whose bark contains quinine, which helps to fight malaria; copal, whose resin is burned as incense to the gods; and large cedar trees, whose trunks are hollowed out to make canoes. Here, too, the chicozapote tree is found—its resin sets like rubber and its fruits, chicos, have a pleasant flavor.

The Mayan rulers are regarded as divine and are revered by their people. The jaguar is the symbol of status and strength, and a totem animal believed to be the envoy of the Lord of the Kingdom of Death. The jaguar's skin is used by the rulers and the priests in rites, during which animals and humans are sacrificed at the foot of the temple.

Back in the present, more than a millennium after Tikal's golden years, we are surrounded by mysterious ruins that were hacked and dug painstakingly out of the forest by archaeologists during the twentieth century. No one knows for sure what happened around 900CE. Perhaps the increasingly intensive cultivation rendered the soil barren; perhaps the sacrificial rites and Mayan way of life degenerated; or perhaps there was a tribal war, which led to Tikal being abandoned suddenly.

The ravages of time have taken their toll. The jungle vegetation moved in with explosive force, ate its way into this monument of Mayan culture, and broke down the limestone with the help of its roots and humus acids. Nature became the conqueror, taking charge several hundred years before the Spanish conquistadors arrived. Lianas, mahogany and kapok trees, climbing plants such as monstera, philodendron, bromeliads, and a whole series of endemic species of plants and animals all compete for space.

The forest's diversity makes Tikal highly prized from a nature conservation point of view. The historic remains of the most splendid Mayan temple-city lend the area another importance, making it doubly valuable as both a cultural and a natural heritage site.

TIKAL

REGISTERED: 1979. Natural
and cultural heritage.
COUNTRY: Guatemala.
FORM OF CONSERVATION: National
park, national monument,
biosphere reserve.
CRITERIA: Ecology,
threatened species.
SIZE: 4,275 square miles
(11,071sq km).
ALTITUDE: 1,970 feet (600m)
above sea level.
LANDSCAPE: River plains with
lagoons and wetlands in a
gently rolling area with
limestone and dolomite bedrock
from the Tertiary era. In the
north, low hills; centrally,
higher hills with steep cliffs.
VEGETATION: 20% of the area
covered in tropical rainforest,
containing more than 2,000
plant species typical of
mountain and lowland forest,
savanna, and wetland. More
than 300 species of useful trees,
such as mahogany, cedar,
breadfruit, and pepper.
FAUNA: 54 mammal species, such
as howler and spider monkeys,
vulnerable giant anteaters
and Baird's tapirs, peccaries,
white-nosed coatis, otters,
and jaguars. Just over 330 bird
species from 63 families, such
as ocellated turkeys, scarlet
macaws, and jabiru storks.
38 snake species, 9 species
of amphibians, and 6 species of
tortoises. Rich variety of fish.
CULTURAL HISTORY: 3,000 buildings
from an ancient Mayan city,
believed to have been inhabited
by 90,000 people at the end of
the 9th century CE.
CONSERVATION VALUE: Temple ruins
and the surrounding forest.
Many vulnerable animal and
plant species. An important part
of the "green corridor" through
Central America.
TOURISM: Most important
site for 15% of tourists
to Guatemala.

GALÁPAGOS
—DARWIN'S ISLANDS

Red "Sally lightfoot" crabs.

The lava cactus is the
first plant to take root
when lava petrifies.

IT IS A REMARKABLE EXPERIENCE to visit the Galápagos Islands 165 years after Charles Darwin's voyage with the frigate *Beagle*, and it is a privilege to be able to watch the descendants of the finches, mockingbirds, and reptiles that stimulated Darwin's ideas about the evolution of species through natural selection. These are the islands that helped to turn the theory of creation upside down, and change our view of the world.

On the sandy beaches we can still meet sea lions basking, just as others had done in Darwin's time, and they accept us and play with us under the water. The greatest experience on the Galápagos is the animals' trust in humans. Fur seals or "sea bears" crawl up the rocks. We see the black Darwin's finches landing on the *Opuntia* cactuses and little Galápagos penguins diving into the sea. Giant turtles drag themselves puffing and panting through the brush, while black sea iguanas bask in groups on the equally black lava rocks. They are the Earth's only species of marine lizard.

"These islands appear paradises for the whole family of reptiles," wrote Darwin of the Galápagos, after his journey in 1835. In fact, there are not that many different species here, but there are large populations of them. The reptiles' body temperature adjusts according to the temperature of their surroundings, and they are therefore more energy-efficient than mammals and can thrive in barren environments with little food. The biggest of the reptiles is the giant tortoise, *Chelonoidis elephantopus*—the eldest specimens could actually be the same individuals that Darwin observed. Each island has its own subspecies of these impressive animals. The largest island—Isabela (Albemarle)—alone is the home of five subspecies, each living on its own volcano.

However, above all, it was the finches on the various Galápagos islands—thirteen species with different-shaped beaks and different food preferences—that helped Darwin to arrive at his theory that species adapt to their environment. He came to many of his conclusions only years after his voyage, as he began to analyze the wealth of material he had collected. It was twenty-four years before his famous book *On the Origin of Species* was published.

There are many more strange species on the Galápagos Islands. The orangey-yellow land iguanas eat cactus fruit, spines and all. The extraordinary Galápagos cormorant has completely lost its ability to fly, thanks to the absence of predators. The little Galápagos

The great attraction for
visitors is that the
animals display such
unwarranted trust.

The long neck of the giant
tortoise means that it can
reach food higher
off the ground.

Following pages: View from
the top of Bartolomé Island
over Pinnacle Rock
and Santiago.

penguin—the only species of penguin that exists in the tropics—was enticed here from the southern hemisphere by the cold Humboldt Current to enjoy the well-stocked larder. The rich seas also encourage frigatebirds, albatrosses, giant whales, and dolphins. On the rocks sit brown pelicans preening their feathers by pulling them one at a time with their clumsy beaks. The greater flamingo came to the Galápagos from the Caribbean and today there are approximately 300 pairs nesting here.

On Fernandina (Narborough) the volcanic eruptions in 1968 and 1995 laid a fresh layer of lava over the landscape, offering a singular kind of beauty. Silvery skeletons of dead, withered mangrove trees are silhouetted artistically against the black ash. Across the sculptural lava rocks, the bright red "Sally lightfoot" crabs scuttle around on tiptoe.

Bartolomé is one of the youngest islands. On the slopes of volcanic ash there are "pioneering" plants such as the gray tiquilia and the lava cactus *Brachycereus,* whose roots can penetrate small fissures in the lava in search of minerals. The view from Cerro Bartolomé is one of the most beautiful in the archipelago. In the bay below stands the leaning cone of Pinnacle Rock with the lava island of Santiago in the background.

Darwin wrote of the land iguanas on Santiago (James) Island: "we could not for some time find a spot free from their burrows, on which to pitch our tent." Today the yellow iguana has been eradicated from Santiago by rats, goats, pigs, and dogs, which were introduced by humans. Cats, donkeys, cows, horses, various insects and parasites, and around 500 plant species can also be added to the list of alien species. Perhaps the hardest task for the national park management, the Charles Darwin Research Station, and the WWF is to eradicate and prevent the further introduction of non-native species.

The Galápagos were isolated from the world until a Spanish vessel carrying Tomás de Berlanga, the bishop of Panama, drifted here on a sea current in 1535. Precisely 300 years before Darwin's visit, he reported back to his king, "Many of the birds are like those in Spain but they are so stupid that they don't even know how to flee." Berlanga called the Galápagos "Las Islas Encantadas"—the enchanted islands.

Until the national park was established in 1959, many species continued to die out. Those lost include the giant rats on Santa Cruz; the great land finches and barn owls on Floreana; the geckos, rice rats, and land iguanas on Rábida; three species of native

The land iguana eats cactus —spines, and all.

The blue-footed booby revealing the obvious reason it was given its name.

One of the thirteen species of "Darwin's finches" found in the islands.

After diving, marine iguanas spray out excess salt, which dries into salt crusts on their heads.

rats on Isabela; land iguanas on Baltra and Santiago; and giant tortoises on Fernandina, Santa Fé, Floreana, and Pinta.

In the nineteenth century whalers killed tens of thousands of fur seals around the islands. Reporting on the sea iguanas, a ship's captain wrote that one "could slaughter several hundred without any problem." The whalers also took over 100,000 tortoises, as a source of fresh meat for sea voyages. There were originally fourteen species of giant tortoise, but three are now extinct. Of a fourth species, native to the island of Pinta, only the celebrated Lonesome George lives on, at the Charles Darwin Research Station.

Thankfully today's tourists are not an acute threat, because they keep to marked paths and are always accompanied by a guide. But increased numbers of human visitors has affected the ecosystems, including the unwitting introduction of non-native species.

The Galápagos triggered Darwin's revolutionary speculation on biogeography and evolution and, with their extraordinary wildlife, the islands are a potent symbol of the natural world. The islands were one of the first places to be designated a World Heritage site, being listed in 1978.

GALÁPAGOS

REGISTERED: 1978.

COUNTRY: Ecuador.

FORM OF CONSERVATION: National park, biosphere reserve.

CRITERIA: Geology, ecology, natural beauty, threatened species.

SIZE: land, 2,960 square miles (7,665sq km), sea 30,850 square miles (79,900sq km).

ALTITUDE: 0–5,600 feet (0–1,707m) above sea level.

LANDSCAPE: 14 large islands, about 115 smaller islands, all volcanic, up to 3–4 million years old. Crater lakes, sulfur and lava fields. Warm, tropical current meets the cold Humboldt Current from Peru.

VEGETATION: 625 species of native plants; at least 500 introduced plants, such as guava, citrus fruits, and elephant grass.

FAUNA: 6 native land mammals, 300 fish species, 1,000 insect species, and 57 native bird species. Endemic species: 46% of seabirds, 75% of land birds, and 100 % of reptiles.

CULTURAL HISTORY: Thought to have been discovered by the Incas in the 15th century. Rediscovered by the Spanish in 1535.

CONSERVATION VALUE: Unique species, high endemism, unusual character of the islands. Exceptional possibilities for biological and evolutionary research.

TOURISM: 63,000 visitors per year (1997).

THREATS: Immigration, illegal fishing, and the spread of non-native species, but not yet on the list of threatened sites.

EUROPE

Europe is the smallest continent after Australia, covering a fifth of the major landmass of Eurasia. South of the narrow strip of tundra up near the Arctic Ocean, coniferous forests predominate, changing to broad-leaved woodland south of the Baltic Sea, with more evergreen vegetation along the Mediterranean coast. The most prominent mountain chains are the Caucasus, the Alps, and the Pyrenees. Within the "old world" continents, particularly Europe, the proportion of cultural sites is very high and six sites are a combination of cultural and natural heritage. But, although large areas have been cultivated and developed, there is a good deal of untouched countryside left. Just under half the twenty-six natural heritage sites have been designated for ecological reasons, while many have been chosen for their geological value and some solely for their beautiful scenery. Here, we describe the mountains of Laponia, the Pyrenees, and bird-rich Doñana.

LAPONIA
—LINNAEUS'S MOUNTAIN LANDSCAPE

The fall colors are vivid—
perhaps most striking on
dogwood bush.

The wooded Muddus region
is extensive, with lakes,
bogs, and dimpled hills.

PADJELANTA IS THE LAND OF WIDE OPEN SPACES, a mountainous region with restful contours in its low mountain ridges and the glassy depths of its big lakes. Here, we tread in the footsteps of Carl von Linné (Linnaeus) and ramble far and wide through a timeless landscape. In the diary of his famous journey to what was then called Lapland in 1732, Linné wrote: "The water in Virihaure Lake was greenish-white and just like water standing in a bowl from which milk has been poured." This stunningly beautiful lake, which has remained untouched, displays precisely the same colors to us nearly 270 years later, and although it was a far greater undertaking to travel here in Linné's time, the lake is still remote today. And that is what is so amazing—that Laponia still has such a large and extensive wild landscape, the largest in Europe outside Russia.

The enormous size of the area means that it is extremely rich in wildlife. During our hike over Padjelanta's heaths we are seduced by the tranquillity of the undulating landscape and the lakes that reflect the light of the sky like wide coastal bays. On Skierfe Mountain, on the edge of Sarek, we see a different view. Beneath the breathtaking 2,300-foot (700m) high southern face lies the Rapa Delta with its jigsaw of meandering streams, which have divided the land into lush, grassy fens, and lagoons of shifting hues. What we see is a multicolored painting, gracefully filling out the molded shape of the valley framed between the three mountains. The streams empty their sediment-laden, turquoise-blue waters into a lake that is shrinking at a rate of 16 feet (5m) per year. Here, if anywhere, the landscape is changing naturally and visibly. The land is alive.

We find a similar mosaic of watercourses farther along the same valley, where the Rapaselet is shadowed by mountains that are higher and more rugged than those at the gateway to the valley. The lake, which once filled the trough, has been obliterated and the meandering streams have rounded off sandbanks and built islands. The silt has laid fertile foundations, creating soil that has allowed the vegetation to grow dense and tangled. With its rich birchwoods, tall rocky fortresses, and deep-cut valley, this is the most splendid location in Laponia.

All around stand Sarek's snow-capped fells, an Arctic world of precipices and glaciers. This is Europe's wildest mountain kingdom, accessible only by people who can withstand rough going in a landscape plagued by stormy weather. The rock has

been chiseled away by inland ice and has steep walls, narrow ridges, and enormous seas of boulders. Up there the rivers collect water and glacial silt. It is a barren environment, which is counterbalanced by the two major valleys of the region—Rapadalen and Njåtjosvagge—rich in wildlife, where Europe's biggest elk live, protected from hunting, and where bears, wolverines, and lynxes are seen regularly.

Sarek was first charted at the end of the nineteenth century. One man more than any other—the geographer Axel Hamberg—made the area known, and when Sweden's first national parks were designated in 1909 it was natural that Sarek should be included. The group included the area around the Stora Sjöfallet, where there was a unique waterfall which even then had begun to attract the tourists. It was described as a wall of falling water that plunged down from a lake straight into a narrow mountain cleft. The waterfall is reported to have been unusually spectacular, but this gem began to dwindle ten years later as a result of water regulation, and today it is merely a trickle. Two big rivers have been dammed to produce hydroelectric power, and they lie like a lost enclave right in the middle of Laponia.

To the east the landscape is gentler and Laponia changes from an alpine mountain range to a tranquil upland plain in which the curves of scattered hilltops stand out. Here the taiga (subarctic coniferous forest) grows uninterrupted and untouched for mile after mile. The landscape is as empty of people as the mountainous areas are, but the scenery that awaits us is different. We walk through the forest in Muddus National Park and follow along the water's edge to a deep cleft, which was carved out by the meltwater of the Ice Age. After about 12 miles (20km), we reach a large area of marshland where the light, spring evenings echo with the sound of whooper swans, jack snipe, and cranes.

We find Europe's largest bog, with even richer birdlife, in the biggest Swedish reserve—Sjaunja—which encompasses the borderland between the taiga and the fells, where the pine forest meets the low-growing birch forest. This mixture of environments creates conditions for an unusual abundance of fauna, such as golden eagles and white-tailed eagles. Both Sjaunja and Muddus lie on the Baltic primary rock shield and have ancient masses of stone, mostly granite. Fifty million years ago, the surface of the land was severely weathered, with only the hardest rocks withstanding erosion.

The fell rocks are of a considerably later date, but even so this mountain chain is one of the oldest on Earth. Just over 500 million years ago the seabed, far to the west, rose up and large plates of sedimentary rock and volcanic magma were pushed in over the bedrock shield. The plate settled horizontally and where the rock was of softer schist it was broken down into an undulating terrain of the kind we see in Padjelanta. Where instead the primary rock contained black amphibolite, it was more resistant and precipitous peaks were chiseled out to form Sarek.

When the World Heritage site was established, the whole of this huge area, including four national parks and two nature reserves, was named Laponia. The area was once the territory of the people known as the Lapps (Saami) and was therefore acknowledged also as a cultural heritage site. We are not sure how long they have lived here, but we do know that during the sixteenth century the Lapps made the transition from hunting reindeer to farming them. As nomads, the Lapps drove their herds from summer pastureland in the fells to their winter grazing in the forests. The reindeer farmers today live in a fixed place, but their reindeer still migrate, just as they did in Linné's time.

LAPONIA

REGISTERED: 1996.
Natural and cultural heritage.
COUNTRY: Sweden.
FORM OF CONSERVATION:
4 national parks,
2 nature reserves.
CRITERIA: Geology, ecology,
natural beauty.
SIZE: 3,490 square miles
(9,040sq km).
ALTITUDE: About 490–6,560
feet (150–2,000m) above
sea level.
LANDSCAPE: To the west, open
low hills with large lakes.
The central parts comprise
an alpine and heavily broken
terrain of high fells with
about 100 glaciers. This
changes in the east into an
extensive and plateau-like
woodland with large bogs
and scattered, rounded hills.
VEGETATION: The low fells are
dominated by heath and
meadows, with just a few
endemic plants, such as
Scandinavian primroses.
The valleys of the high
fells are covered with alpine
birch woods, which form the
treeline and also spread over
the flatter terrain east of
the fells. The eastern parts
have extensive wooded
areas, consisting largely
of virgin forests of pine and
fir. The wetlands comprise
alternately moss and marsh
vegetation. 600 vascular
plants recorded.
FAUNA: 25 different mammals
and 100 species of nesting
birds. High incidence of bears
and lynxes, and established
stocks of threatened animals
such as wolverines, otters,
and white-tailed eagles.
In the valleys there are
Europe's biggest elk.
Small game such as red
foxes, martens, stoats,
and hares are common.
Golden eagles, gyr falcons,
and peregrine falcons nest
here regularly. Willow grouse
and ptarmigan are common.
Large population of
whooper swans.
CULTURAL HISTORY: The area
is the homeland of Saami
(Lapp) reindeer farmers.
There are migratory tracks
for the reindeer, temporary
settlements and places
of great significance to
the Saami culture.
CONSERVATION VALUE:
Spectacular landscape of
outstanding beauty: virgin
forests, lakes, and watercourses. Great biological
diversity. Well-preserved
natural environment for many
globally threatened species.
TOURISM: 10,000 visitors
per year.

THE PYRENEES
—THE FLORAL MOUNTAINS

Short-leaved gentians cling
to the high slopes.

Spain's Ordesa Valley is an
inspiring sight from the
Faja de Pelay trail.

ON THE SPANISH SIDE OF THE PYRENEAN MOUNTAIN CHAIN WE VISIT the impressive Ordesa Valley, a deep-cut canyon which can compare with any of the great gorges of the world. The sides are 3,280 feet (1,000m) high, and resemble a fortress, rising abruptly. The valley is often called Europe's Grand Canyon, although it is considerably smaller in size than the American canyon of that name, and the vegetation here is much more luxuriant, thanks to the humid climate and fertile soil. In the bottom of the valley there is a dense, broad-leaf forest of beech and Pyrenean oak. In the clearings we see an abundance of plants, such as Turk's head lilies and colorful saxifrages, primulas, and gentians. Higher up, the coniferous trees take over—first common pine, then both pine and silver spruce.

Until 1802, when the explorer Ramon de Carbonnières came here, the Ordesa Valley was virtually unknown, and almost 100 years went by after his visit before the area was mapped precisely. In 1918 it was designated a national park, one of the first to be established in Europe. The valley has only one entrance, to the west, and its long arc ends in a cauldron-shaped area, where cattle graze. In the scree below the precipices flocks of pyrenean chamois gambol. Above the basin rises Mont Perdu, which, at 11,000 feet (3,353m), is the third highest peak in the chain. It is a vast mountain with delightful rock veining. On its northern side, out of sight of the valley, lies a very small glacier.

The Pyrenees are young mountains, the same age as the Alps. They were formed during two folding periods, the last of which occurred around fifty million years ago. The central peaks consist largely of hard granite and gneiss, while limestone dominates the mountains farther out, giving the landscape a light color.

North of the Ordesa Valley lie the highest mountains, which form a natural frontier with France, while on the other side the mountain chain drops more steeply down to lowlands. Here, in 1967, the French government created a long, narrow national park, 43 miles (70km) long and about three miles (5km) wide, that follows the highest ridge of the Pyrenees. The main attraction is the enormous mountain basin of Gavarnie, a glacial cirque carved out by ice masses through the ages. The result is a natural, semicircular amphitheater with 4,265-feet (1,300m) high rock walls, which on one side has a waterfall, 1,475 feet (450m) high. This singular place is visited every year by many tourists who walk or ride in the valleys and climb the mountains.

Beyond Gavarnie the Pyrenees unfold to both east and west. Farther west the French national park is crossed by one of the few roads which traverse the range. Close by is an isolated and slender peak—the Pic du Midi d'Ossau—which is 9,460 feet (2,884m) high. As early as 1787 an expedition tried to establish the height of this mountain, but its members never reached the top. This privilege fell to a shepherd, a few years later. In the mid-nineteenth century the area was explored by the eccentric Count Henry Russell, who became a legend because of his love of the precipitous mountain, Vignemale. For a long time he lived, and held feasts, in a cave in the massif below Vignemale's little glacier.

North of Vignemale we walk to the Lac de Gaube, which nestles in a landscape that reflects the Pyrenees in microcosm. Along the slopes nearest the water there are pinewoods. Between the tops of the trees two headlands and rock promontories protrude, and from the valley beyond the lake the steep, high snow-capped peaks rise majestically. This mountain chain creates a rugged impression and we can easily understand how it long formed an insurmountable barrier between France and Spain.

THE PYRENEES

REGISTERED: 1997. Natural and cultural heritage.

COUNTRY: Spain–France.

FORM OF CONSERVATION: 2 national parks.

CRITERIA: Geology, natural beauty.

SIZE: 118 square miles (306sq km), of which 77 square miles (201sq km) are in Spain.

ALTITUDE: 1,970–11,000 feet (600–3,352m) above sea level.

LANDSCAPE: Alpine mountain area with 4 cauldron-like glacier niches on the northern side. Three deep canyons cut through the southern side. The bedrock consists largely of limestone with some granite.

VEGETATION: Broad-leaf woodland with Pyrenean oak and beech; at higher levels coniferous trees. More than 1,500 flowering plants, a fifth of which are unique to the Pyrenees.

FAUNA: The marmot has been reintroduced. Common mammals are roe deer, wild boar, and predators such as stoats, genets, and badgers. There are approximately 800 Pyrenean chamois, and some ibexes. Bears are seen sporadically. One endemic species is the Pyrenean desman. Among the birds are lammergeiers, peregrine falcons, Bonelli's eagles, and ptarmigans.

CULTURAL HISTORY: The oldest traces of humans date back 40,000 years. On the mountain slopes there is old-fashioned terracing.

CONSERVATION VALUE: The landscape's wealth of geophysical shapes is unique. Spectacular canyons and glacier niches. During the Ice Age the higher sections formed an ice-free area where plants and animals took refuge, and in this way they developed into endemic species.

TOURISM: 2 million visitors per year.

DOÑANA
—ELDORADO FOR MIGRATORY BIRDS

Large numbers of greylag geese from Scandinavia and Germany seek their winter refuge in Doñana's wetlands.

Sand dunes, pines, cork oaks, and marshes border the shore.

WHERE THE SEA ENDS, DOÑANA BEGINS. The Atlantic Ocean surges up with deep breaths and exhales in long-drawn sighs against the beach, over the feet of the sanderlings hurrying after tiny crustaceans and other invertebrates. On the landward side the sand continues in even higher waves, a little Sahara whose rolling dunes are stopped short by a forest of pine trees. We travel in a four-wheel-drive vehicle through grassy plains, bushy heaths, cork oaks full of herons, storks, and small birds, along the edge of *las marismas*— the swamps where tens of thousands of Scandinavian greylag geese and ducks gather in winter. Deer and wild boar emerge from the forest at dusk. We can also sense the presence of the threatened Spanish lynx, and of the rare Spanish imperial eagle, which has perhaps just caught sight of us from some treetop.

The land has been named after Doña Ana, a seventeenth-century lady married to the seventh duke of Medina-Sidonia, whose family owned the forests and the marsh for half a millennium. Doñana became a national park in 1969, but threats from settlement, agriculture, and toxic discharges still hang heavy over this Eldorado for migratory birds.

DOÑANA

REGISTERED: 1994.
COUNTRY: Spain.
FORM OF CONSERVATION: National park, biosphere reserve.
CRITERIA: Ecology, natural beauty, threatened species.
SIZE: 300 square miles (773sq km).
ALTITUDE: 0–130 feet (0–40m) above sea level.
LANDSCAPE: Extensive wetland around the estuary of the Guadalquivir. Marshlands—*las marismas*—on clay soil with canals and waterholes. Sand dunes.

VEGETATION: In damp areas heather plants of the genus *Erica*. On the dry ground marram grass, lavender, pines, and cork oaks. Marsh vegetation varies depending on the level of salt present. Reeds in the freshwater areas. 750 species of vascular plants recorded.
FAUNA: 30 mammals, such as wild boar, deer, otters, genets, Egyptian mongooses, and wild cats. Population of about 40 lynxes. Extremely rich in birds—365 species

have been recorded. Overwintering site for large flocks of greylag geese, teals, wigeons, and avocets. 20,000 flamingos in *las marismas*. White-headed ducks, marbled teals, and imperial eagles are rare.
CULTURAL HISTORY: Old hunting ground for the Spanish kings.
CONSERVATION VALUE: One of Europe's biggest wetlands with a large number of nesting birds. Important stopover site in winter for European migratory birds.
TOURISM: 250,000 visitors per year.

AFRICA

Africa is the continent of wide, grassy plains called savannas, which benefit from alternating dry and rainy seasons. South of the Sahara Desert different types of savanna follow on seamlessly from one another, from Guinea in West Africa to the tip of South Africa, only interrupted by the rainforest of Central Africa and the desert steppes of the Kalahari. A third of all natural heritage sites are in Africa, most registered because of threatened species. In East Africa, the grasslands of the Serengeti and the plains of Ngorongoro offered us encounters with a singularly rich and untouched variety of wildlife. We had the privilege of standing on the peaks of mountains selected for their natural beauty and not their geology. We climbed Africa's two highest mountains, Kilimanjaro and Mount Kenya, crossed game reserves, experienced the continent's biggest waterfall, and visited the three western Indian Ocean islands that have natural heritage sites.

SERENGETI
—THE ENDLESS PLAINS

Lappet-faced vultures perch
on a tree, alert for carrion.

Twice a year storms come
to the Serengeti: from
March to May and from
November to December.

Following pages: Giraffes
grow over 16 feet (5m) tall
and may weigh up to 4,400
pounds (2,000kg).

THE TREMENDOUS UNDULATING MOVEMENT of grassy expanse merges with the sky into a narrow band, far away on the horizon. Our dream of Africa is coming true. This is how the landscape must have looked where primitive man evolved into modern man.

Farther to the north the plain becomes a fertile savanna, with groves of trees, shrubs, and denser vegetation. Softly rounded hills provide a restful backdrop to this area. In contrast, strange little rocky islands look as if they have been thrown down from the sky, but they are all that is left of the weathered primary rock. These so-called *kopje* were embedded in ash after the eruption of the volcanoes on the Ngorongoro uplands. Many consist of boulders as big as houses, while others are embedded slabs, and more still rise as steep massifs almost 200 feet (60m) high. The klipspringer and the agama lizard thrive here, and the rocks are popular haunts of lions too.

The name of this, the biggest of Tanzania's national parks, comes from the Masai word *siringet*, which means "endless plain." In the southeastern part the plain lies bare for 15–25 miles (25–40km) and it is here that the enormous herds of wildebeests (or gnus) gather for calving in December and January. The interaction between the animals and the vegetation in the Serengeti is at the root of one of the animal world's biggest spectacles—the annual migration of millions of wildebeests, zebras, and gazelles.

After their calving in the east, where the soil is thin and the grass short, the herds move to the western plains where the earth is richer, the rain heavier (and the grass therefore higher), and the copses more prevalent. Many animals go as far as Lake Victoria, outside the boundaries of the park. When the food withers during the dry season between June and October, they are forced to move farther north to the rolling uplands of the Masai Mara reserve in Kenya, which at that time still has flourishing vegetation. In endless, noisy columns the animals move like soldiers on the march between the savanna's scattered acacia trees. A dramatic scene is played out as masses of animals take over the Mara River, where crocodiles float like logs as they wait for their prey. In December the herds return south and in the course of nine months they have roamed clockwise around a triangle within this enormous ecosystem of 35,000 square miles (90,650sq km). The great predators are their constant companions. Almost 2,000 lions roam this area, which is the world's richest in wildlife.

Serengeti has a large population of cheetahs—the world's fastest land animals over short distances.

Acacia trees grow on the volcanic earth.

Wildebeests and zebras often mingle in the large herds.

But it has not always been thus. Toward the end of the nineteenth century wildebeest stocks were heavily depleted by a disease that originated from the Masai's domesticated cattle. In the 1920s, when the Serengeti became famous among hunters, safaris were organized for groups, which sometimes shot hundreds of lions. The number of big cats was so drastically reduced that the central part of the area was designated a wildlife reserve in 1929. Just twenty years later the national park was formed.

Today the park is under pressure from the surrounding human population. In some places there are small fortifications where park wardens are stationed. As early as 1978 Tanzania established an armed organization to combat poaching, but in spite of that only a handful of rhinoceroses are left in the Serengeti, and these are now fitted with radio transmitters—a new weapon in the defense arsenal. The elephants are also threatened by poachers and in recent years more and more animals have been seeking shelter in the northern parts of the park. In spite of these problems, a visit to the Serengeti is an overwhelming experience. One sees one species of animal after another in an area, which, more than any other, is truly the kingdom of the animals.

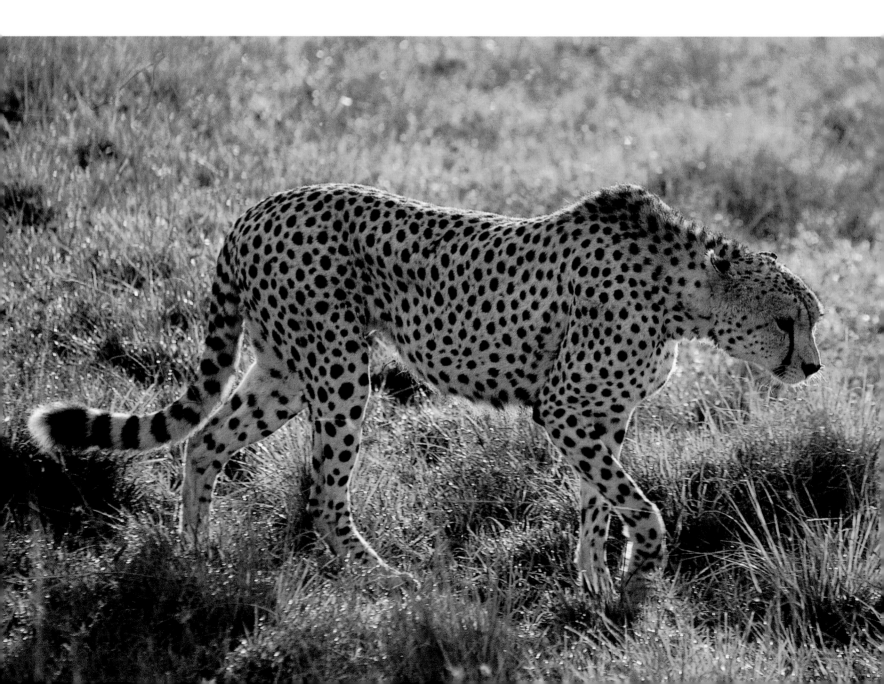

SERENGETI

REGISTERED: 1981.

COUNTRY: Tanzania.

FORM OF CONSERVATION: National park, biosphere reserve.

CRITERIA: Natural beauty, threatened species.

SIZE: 5,700 square miles (14,763sq km).

ALTITUDE: 3,018–6,070 feet (920–1,850 m) above sea level.

LANDSCAPE: Broad plains on volcanic ash. Quantities of small granite rocks scattered like islands in a sea of grass. In the north and west, extensive mountain ridges of volcanic origin. Two river systems with tributaries that flow west; small lakes, marshes, and watering holes.

VEGETATION: The plains are dominated by millet and *Sporobolus* grass. In damper areas another species of grass takes over. The central parts consist of broad savannas, sparsely populated with the umbrella acacia and, to some extent, the *Commiphora* tree. In the north a good deal of bush vegetation.

FAUNA: Almost 1.5 million wildebeests, 1 million gazelles, 200,000 zebras. Most of Africa's big predators: about 2,000 lions, 500 leopards, and large numbers of hyenas. Also cheetahs and African wild dogs, which are a threatened species. 500 bird species recorded.

CULTURAL HISTORY: Formerly inhabited by the Masai and their cattle, now devoid of people apart from administrative personnel and others who work in the national park.

CONSERVATION VALUE: The richest area of wildlife in the world. The savanna has a complex ecosystem with herds of grazing animals and predators.

TOURISM: 200,000 visitors per year.

NGORONGORO

—A PLAYGROUND FOR WILDLIFE

The Masai live in their traditional way outside the crater.

A bank of cloud drifts in over the forested crater rim.

Following pages: Elephants in the Lerai Forest with "freeloading" cattle egrets.

WHEN THE SUN RISES behind the wall of the mountains, the crater is bathed in light like a gigantic, shimmering bowl. The views alone make Ngorongoro a magnificent sight and yet it is not primarily for the majestic scenery that we have come here. It is down there in the bottom of the crater that unique experiences await us. In this deep, broad basin we shall meet a world which is literally bubbling over with wildlife, an unlikely melting pot where 20,000 large mammals are gathered on a rolling 15-mile (24-km) plain, encircled by a high rock wall all the way round the basin's horizon. It is a world so concentrated, so alive, so luxuriant that it could be Noah's ark beached on grass. There is nothing like it anywhere else.

The eighth wonder of the world, as Ngorongoro Crater is often called, originated fifteen million years ago, when the area was being shaped by volcanic activity. Earthquakes and powerful movements occurred all along the African rift. Lava built up volcanoes and the ash from their eruptions spread westward, where the fertile soil of the Serengeti plain was laid, at the same time as traces of the first primitive humans were buried and preserved in Olduvai Gorge.

Two and a half million years ago Ngorongoro was probably a volcano of the same height as Kilimanjaro, but when its pipe became blocked the magma found other ways out. The cone developed cracks and cavities within and collapsed into an enormous caldera—an imploded crater. Through this dramatic natural phenomenon the volcano was extinguished and the vegetation moved in. With the greenery came animals, and then nature created its own zoo, enclosed not within a fence but within an almost 2,000-feet (610-m) high rock wall, which forms the backdrop to the herds.

On the grass plain in this enclosed world there is a marsh rich in birdlife and a soda lake with flamingos. Large numbers of wildebeests and zebras graze on the open spaces. A visible gallery of forest with slender fever acacia grows close to the rock wall, and the high ridge of the crater is covered with dense rainforest. For the elephants the rock wall is a physical problem and the calves cannot manage to scale it. Down in the crater there are only bulls, often with remarkably large tusks, while the cows and calves remain outside Ngorongoro. Most species of animal stay here all year round. Some migration to and fro occurs across the crater walls, which can reach over 7,000 feet (2,130m), but

A large herd of
wildebeests and zebras
grazing peacefully.

The elegant gray crowned
crane often roams in flocks.

the supply of new blood may be too small. The number of lions has dwindled considerably and is now down to twenty, possibly owing to inbreeding.

The crater is one of the last havens for the severely threatened black rhinoceros, thanks to the fact that the park wardens have a good view over this well-defined area. They check all vehicles moving among the animals and we have to leave the crater before dusk. There is a proposal to limit the number of vehicles to a maximum of fifty per day to reduce disruption. Tourism has become a threat to the Earth's biggest caldera, but the crater comprises only 3 percent of the whole World Heritage site, which also includes seven other extinct volcanoes.

The Ngorongoro nature reserve was formed in the 1950s as an offshoot of the Serengeti National Park. Today, around 42,000 Masai live in the conservation area and the authorities endeavor to combine wildlife conservation with the Masai's pastoral herding culture. It is a difficult balancing act because the Masai are not allowed to graze their cattle in the crater. We can only hope that Ngorongoro will always remain the Garden of Eden that Mother Nature created.

NGORONGORO

REGISTERED: 1979.

COUNTRY: Tanzania.

FORM OF CONSERVATION: Nature conservation area, biosphere reserve.

CRITERIA: Ecology, natural beauty, threatened species.

SIZE: 3,125 square miles (8,094sq km), of which the crater is 102 square miles (264sq km).

ALTITUDE: 4,920–11,970 feet (1,500–3,648 m) above sea level.

LANDSCAPE: To the west open plains with fault cracks such as Olduvai Gorge. To the east a volcanic massif with the gigantic crater of Ngorongoro and several smaller craters.

VEGETATION: Rainforest and brush cover the steep mountainsides. Rolling grass plains in Ngorongoro's crater and plains to the west of the volcano.

FAUNA: Particularly high incidence of wildebeests and zebras. Rich in birdlife such as flamingos and pelicans.

CULTURAL HISTORY: The Olduvai Gorge has fossils of early man. The Masai tribespeople live in the area.

CONSERVATION VALUE: The world's largest inactive caldera, with African big game including the threatened black rhinoceros.

TOURISM: 120,000 visitors per year.

KILIMANJARO
—A MIRAGE IN THE SKY

Climbers with a board
proclaiming that they have
reached the highest
point in Africa.

In the twilight the cloud lifts
a little and a giant *Senecio*
emerges eerily against the
backdrop of the mighty
Barranco wall.

Following pages: Climbers
on Kibo's crater rim with
Mawenzi in the background.

WHAT DID JOHANNES REBMANN THINK OF KILIMANJARO when he looked up at the roof of Africa from the savanna in 1848? How can a mountain top hover in the sky? We are certainly dumbfounded when the "white queen" emerges from the cloud. There is little else to rival the contrast between Kilimanjaro's lofty elevation and the flat plain that surrounds it. With a height difference from top to toe of just over 16,400 feet (5,000m), this big, solitary landmark is visible from farther away than any other mountain on Earth.

After hiking for four days and a night in the increasingly thin air, we reach the summit. Up here the air pressure is only half that at sea level and our lack of oxygen contributes to the dreamlike quality of the experience.

Part of the time we are walking over snow and come close to some of the twelve glaciers that weigh down the slopes. They look strange—pale blocks against the dark lava, some reminiscent of stepped terraces. The intense ultraviolet rays combined with the sun beaming down directly over the equator are melting them "vertically" and the glaciers are acquiring a startling, almost cubist, appearance.

Rebmann and another German missionary were the first Europeans to reach the foot of Kilimanjaro. He wrote of the white peak in his diary: "The most wonderful memory ran through my head, that this was a familiar old European guest called snow." In Europe the discovery caused uproar. Geographers claimed that he had seen limestone, not snow, but today we know that such high peaks have their own cool climate even on the equator. Nights up there easily drop below 14°F (-10°C) and the temperature rises as quickly as the sun. Banks of cloud build up in the morning and, as a rule, form a dense carpet below 14,760 feet (4,500m).

Kilimanjaro's symmetrical cone has a cut-off profile. From the highest point we look down into a great crater, which no one standing at the foot of the mountain would suspect existed—a secret world, one and a half miles (2.4km) in diameter, and encircled by a rock wall up to 650 feet (200m) high. Two smaller craters lie inside one another, down below. In the innermost, which cannot be seen from the top of the mountain, a smouldering sulfur spring reveals that volcanic activity has not quite died out.

The mountain was born a million years ago from the Great Rift Valley, the constantly moving continental rift that stretches between the Red Sea and Lake Malawi.

Liquid magma poured out from three hot holes in the ground and created three volcanoes. The middle one grew into Kilimanjaro's famous Kibo crater. The most westerly, Shira, collapsed into a caldera. When the most easterly fire-hole died out, the crater was gradually worn down, leaving behind a hard magma plug, which today forms Kibo's steep twin peak, Mawenzi.

During our climb we pass a series of different vegetation belts which garland the mountain. First, a dense and lush mountain rainforest of the *Podocarpus* and *Nuxia* genera of trees. Higher up, park-like heaths open out, with groves of slender tree heathers. The vegetation becomes increasingly sparse and finally it is replaced by sterile lava fields, with huge boulders bordering the path. In the valleys along the Marangu and Machame trails the tall afro-alpine rosette plants of the *Lobelia* and *Senecio* genera grow. Sunbirds can sometimes be seen hovering between the big leaves.

All climbers on Kilimanjaro must use accredited guides. In this way a check can be kept on the impact of tourists on the environment. But on the whole Kilimanjaro has a strong defense in the form of its own barren landscape and thin atmosphere.

KILIMANJARO

REGISTERED: 1989.

COUNTRY: Tanzania.

FORM OF CONSERVATION: National park.

CRITERIA: Natural beauty.

SIZE: 290 square miles (754sq km).

ALTITUDE: 6,000–19,400 feet (1,830–5,895m) above sea level.

LANDSCAPE: Oval, volcanic massif, 37 miles (60km) long. West and east of Kibo, the highest cone, are plateaus. In the east is Mawenzi, a steep, jagged-edged mountain.

VEGETATION: Rainforest between 6,230 and 9,850 feet (1,900–3,000m). Above that, heath with tufted grasslands, shrubs, and afro-alpine rosette plants. Sparse vegetation above 14,000 feet (4,300m).

FAUNA: Elands and common duikers are found above the treeline. In the forest there are colobus and blue monkeys, and leopards.

CONSERVATION VALUE: Africa's highest mountain and one of the world's highest volcanoes. Unique topographical shapes rising 3 miles (5km) above the surrounding plain.

TOURISM: 12,000 visitors per year.

MOUNT KENYA
—THE ALPINE PEAK OF THE SAVANNA

Mackinder's gladiolus blooms magnificently on the slopes of the mountain.

A rock hyrax rests below Point John in the Teleki Valley.

Following pages: From the Tarn Hut there is just under 2,000 feet (600m) to go to reach Mount Kenya's highest peak.

FROM THE PLAIN BELOW, MOUNT KENYA, 17,040 feet (5,194m) high, is even more intriguing than Kilimanjaro. The mountain is not as high as the "white queen" or "roof of Africa," as Kilimanjaro is known, but stands like a phallus on a domed plinth, which has a diameter of 31 miles (50km). It is the hub of a compact mountain range with ridges several miles long that run out to all points of the compass and are divided from one another by deep valleys. The massif is crowned with seven small glaciers that sparkle like diamonds in the tropical sun before the dense afternoon clouds close in. Most of the glaciers hang suspended on the slopes, but the biggest nestles in a basin of rock.

In 1899 the geographer Halford Mackinder, accompanied by two alpine guides, was the first person to reach the summit of Mount Kenya. He named the highest peak after Batian, a legendary Masai chief, and the next highest, Nelion, after the chief's brother. Nelion is only 30 feet (10m) lower than Batian and they are separated by the 130-feet (40m) gorge, "The Gate of Mists." The third highest peak reaches 16,350 feet (4,985m) and was called Lenana, after Batian's son. This peak is the tourists' goal, while the two taller ones are considered more difficult to climb.

Mount Kenya was possibly the Earth's highest mountain when eruptions were at their greatest, around three million years ago. The volcano that formed then was probably over 23,000 feet (7,000m) high, but when the eruptions ceased it quickly crumbled away, partly because of the abrasive effect of the glaciers. Only the hard plug of magma, which had blocked the chimney, was left. This cracked open vertically and was honed to a sharp peak. The slightly rusty color of the rock causes the rugged massif to glow like a torch in the first light of dawn.

Mount Kenya is considered more treacherous to climb than Kilimanjaro. The most popular route leads quickly up to the higher levels and the thin air. During the climb we pass through a dense rainforest that is rich in wildlife, such as colobus monkeys, giant forest hogs, and bongo antelopes. Around 8,200 feet (2,500m) this becomes a matted bamboo jungle that is peculiar to Mount Kenya and largely absent from Kilimanjaro. The jungle thins out around 9,840 feet (3,000m), where we emerge on to heathland with isolated trees of the genus *Hagenia*. Bushes and tufted grass vegetation dominate here and the ground can be marshy and heavy-going after rain.

Higher up we meet the bizarre *Senecio* trees. They have rosettes of leaves at the top of sturdy stems, 16 to 20 feet (5–6m) high, that consist of old leaf joints. These unique plants are bigger on Mount Kenya than on Kilimanjaro and at between 11,480 and 13,100 feet (3,500–4,000m) they almost form a forest. Another group of rosette plants are the giant lobelias. From a rosette of leaves on the ground they grow a tall stem embellished with small flowers. Of the two species on the mountain, the big ostrich-plume lobelia is the more unusual. The stem can grow to 10 feet (3m) high and has narrow, silvery leaves that stick straight out to keep the night frost at bay. Against the light the whole plant shimmers like a Christmas tree.

Where the rosette plants grow, rock hyraxes also thrive, as they like to eat the fruits. These rodent-like animals hop around on the ground like overgrown guinea pigs, but they are most closely related to the elephants. Apart from rock hyraxes and occasional leopards there is not much wildlife on the higher slopes. But the nectar of the giant flowers does attract shimmering malachite sunbirds, and high up in the sky one may see a lammergeier, or an alpine swift.

MOUNT KENYA

REGISTERED: 1997.

COUNTRY: Kenya.

FORM OF CONSERVATION: National park, forest reserve.

CRITERIA: Ecology, natural beauty.

SIZE: 548 square miles (1,420sq km).

ALTITUDE: 5,250–17,060 feet (1,600–5,199m) above sea level.

LANDSCAPE: Isolated, steeply contoured mountain massif of volcanic origin. Between the ridges deep valleys with occasional, small lakes.

VEGETATION: Several different vegetation belts, changing with increases in altitude. Mountain rainforest, bamboo forest, alpine grass moors with heather. Above the forest unique afro-alpine vegetation with giant rosette plants of the genera *Lobelia* and *Senecio*. Many endemic species.

FAUNA: In the rainforest elephants, "black panthers" (leopards), colobus monkeys, and the timid bongo antelopes. Rock hyraxes typical of the alpine moors. Birds include sunbirds and mountain francolins.

CONSERVATION VALUE: The second highest mountain in Africa and one of the continent's most impressive landscapes. Several threatened species of animal are found in the forests.

TOURISM: 15,000 visitors per year, of whom half reach Point Lenana.

VICTORIA FALLS

—THE SMOKE THAT THUNDERS

The bushbuck is sometimes
seen in the forest
bordering the falls.

In the dry season the
main falls offers a good
view, while in the rainy
season there is an
impenetrable spray.

Following pages: In
Livingstone's time the
Kololo people believed that
the falls was bewitched and
the rainbow was a divine
manifestation.

THERE IS AN EXTREMELY UNNERVING, DIZZY FEELING—our senses are drawn down with the water and spray that swirls toward the bottom of the canyon with dramatic effect. Lying on your stomach and peering fearfully over the edge of the Victoria Falls, where millions of gallons of water hurtle down toward the basalt rocks 350 feet (107m) below, is probably the only way to gauge how Dr. David Livingstone felt 145 years ago.

Here, in 1855, on the side that is now in Zambia, the famous missionary and explorer paddled his canoe, and was utterly amazed by the height and force of the falls. Livingstone saw from a distance how enormous columns of small water droplets rose up toward the sky and how their tops "appeared to mingle with the clouds. They were white below, and higher up became dark, so as to simulate smoke very closely."

Livingstone's canoe was skillfully maneuvered away from the falls by the local people, who took him to an island on the edge. He leaned over the drop and later wrote that "no one could comprehend where this expanse of water went; it seemed to lose itself in the earth, disappear into a lateral fissure." It was also after this experience that he wrote his famous words: "Scenes so lovely must have been gazed upon by angels in their flight."

Others who followed in his wake called the falls "the work of the devil" and many local people kept away from them so as not to disturb the god who was believed to manifest himself in the rainbow. When the sun is out, a rainbow extends over the national frontier, from the main falls in Zambia, across the dizzying abyss to the rainforest on the Zimbabwean side. At the western end of the gorge, Japanese tourists take photographs of each other enthusiastically, in front of a large bronze statue of David Livingstone. Victoria Falls was called Mosi-Oa-Tunya—"the smoke that thunders"—by the Kololo people, long before Livingstone named it after Queen Victoria.

When the wide Zambezi River has reached the bottom of the mile-wide (1.7km) hole in the bedrock, the falls finds its way out through an opening and is led along through a zigzag-shaped canyon, which forms five parallel gorges of the same depth. Earlier discoverers thought there had been some powerful subsidence in the earth's crust, but today researchers believe that the gorges have been carved out by the river's own force over millions of years. Nevertheless, they look as if a giant had formed them by scratching backward and forward in the earth's crust with a stick.

The Zambezi River is known for its large population of hippopotamuses. This one was photographed just above the falls.

The extraordinary, parallel canyons that are found immediately downstream of the falls.

In May, toward the end of the rainy season, about 130 million US gallons (half a billion liters) of water per minute carve their way into the rock. By October, at the end of the dry season, the volume has reduced to about 5 million US gallons (20 million liters) per minute. The spectacle is often called "the biggest curtain of falling water in the world." The Zimbabwean side of the gorge offers the best view, and there the "rainforest" is also resplendent, flourishing in the mists of the falls. It is not really a rainforest, but its moisture and lushness have led to the vegetation being given this popular name.

Here, we find ebony, fig, and mahogany trees—all common along African rivers. Within Africa, the fern *Cheilanthes farinosa* is found only in this forest and two sites in Zambia. Visitors to the falls often see warthogs, monkeys, and bushbuck, and patrolling above the rocks, Verreaux's eagle and the taita falcon. A peaceful way to experience nature here is to take a boat out on the river above the falls at sunset, when elephants and antelopes come down to the riverbank to drink. The silence is broken only by hippopotamuses snorting as they come up to the water's surface to take in some air.

VICTORIA FALLS

REGISTERED: 1989.

COUNTRY: Zambia–Zimbabwe.

FORM OF CONSERVATION:
National park.

CRITERIA: Ecology, natural beauty.

SIZE: 26 square miles (69sq km).

ALTITUDE: 2,725–3,000 feet
(833–915m) above sea level.

LANDSCAPE: During the rainy
season the Victoria Falls has the
world's biggest single curtain of
falling water—the width is just
over a mile (1,700m) and the
height 350 feet (107m). River-
eroded gorges formed in fault
zones in a basalt plateau.

VEGETATION: The forest is
dominated by *Colophospermum
mopane* interspersed with teak,
among other trees. The gallery
forest along the river contains
trees such as acacia, ebony,
olive, and date palms. The
dense undergrowth with ferns
is dependent on the mists
of the falls.

FAUNA: Big game such
as elephants, buffaloes,
wildebeests, zebras, and
giraffes. Hippopotamuses
common above the falls, which
form a topographical boundary
for fish. 84 fish species found
upstream of the falls,
39 downstream.

CULTURAL HISTORY: 3 million-year-
old relics of primitive man,
Homo habilis. 50,000-year-old
stone tools, more recent
Stone Age relics. Livingstone
"discovered" the falls in 1855.

CONSERVATION VALUE: One of the
world's most spectacular
waterfalls; outstanding example
of ongoing river erosion.

TOURISM: One of Africa's
most frequently visited
national parks.

MANA POOLS
—THE WILD ZAMBEZI

The African fish eagle is on the lookout along rivers and lakes all over Africa.

The legendary and life-giving Zambezi River attracts herds of elephants and ungulates during the dry season.

Following pages: Alert and elegant, a Common zebra and foal.

SUDDENLY I SIT BOLT UPRIGHT in bed under the mosquito net as a lion family kills an impala outside my thin-walled tent. The din is aggressive and terrifying. The clock shows three in the morning and it is pitch dark. This natural drama, which makes my blood run cold, is played out just 130 feet (40m) away. The next morning we find nine tired but sated lions—four of them cubs—resting under a nearby acacia.

The experience occurs in Ruckomechi camp in the wild country around Mana Pools, along the Zambezi River. This national park is off the beaten track and we have come to Ruckomechi from Kariba in a little, single-engine Cessna plane. Even as we land, we see something special right beside the airstrip—a cheetah.

The Zambezi Valley spreads out for 30 miles (50km) before it is confined by a steep fault wall. Closer to the river, silt which has built up over thousands of years has created a lowland made up of deposits—alluvial terraces—approximately 2 miles (3km) wide. The fertile terraces are split by former flood channels, which now act as waterholes, attracting large numbers of game when they fill up during the rainy season. Toward the end of the dry season many of these pools have dried out so that we can walk on the cracked mud. In a small, residual puddle little egrets await wetter times.

There is a wealth of wildlife in Mana Pools, Sapi, and Chewore, the three reserves which form the World Heritage site, including elephants, lions, hippopotamuses, African buffaloes, kudus, elands, waterbucks, and zebras. The seriously threatened black rhinoceroses live on here, in the biggest population of them in Africa. Patrols to combat poachers are constantly on the move. There is also a rich variety of birds, with shore-birds, herons, fish eagles, storks, ducks, geese, warblers, and bee-eaters in large numbers.

In the driest part of the year the animals are forced to go down to the river to find water. One day a herd of elephants passes straight through Ruckomechi camp. They stumble along the sandy riverbank and wade through the mat of water hyacinths—a beautiful, unspoilt natural scene. But the damage caused to the acacias in the park by the elephants is evidence of the threat that these animals pose to the ecosystem.

The Zambezi River has one of the densest populations of hippopotamuses and crocodiles in Africa. During a canoe trip with all the camera equipment on board, we feel uneasy about being capsized by an irritated hippopotamus. The area is popular with

A lioness rests after the
night's hunting, which
ended in the middle of the
Ruckomechi camp.

These elephants in the camp
demonstrate how close one
can get to the wild animals
in Mana Pools.

The greater kudu is one of
Africa's biggest and most
beautiful antelopes.

canoeists and many people come here on day trips or week-long canoe safaris. You can go on foot in the park, provided you take care. We walk for long stretches, between rests on the riverbank, through one of the most untamed, natural areas of Zimbabwe.

The Cessna plane carries us on to Chekwenya camp, which has a view over the flood plains. Kudus lift their heads as we stop the jeep a short distance from them, and a saddlebill stork struts as if on stilts among the water hyacinths. The sun is going down across the mystic curves of the Zambezi, coloring the sky and its reflection in the river a deep red. Vultures sit in silhouette at the top of an *Acacia albida*. This tree dominates the riverbanks and is very important to the ecosystem. It bears leaves and up to 880 pounds (400kg) of seedpods during the dry season—precisely when elephants most need both shade and food. Farther away from the river, the mopane forest takes over.

A basking hippopotamus suddenly rises up and half of his fat body becomes visible above the water. He yawns so widely that his jaw seems to be at the brink of dislocation and then he sinks back down under the water with a long sigh. The rings in the water vibrate in the sunset—this is the real Africa in its most soul-stirring incarnation.

MANA POOLS

REGISTERED: 1984.

COUNTRY: Zimbabwe.

FORM OF CONSERVATION:
1 national park, 2 safari areas.

CRITERIA: Ecology, natural beauty, threatened species.

SIZE: 2,611 square miles (6,766sq km).

ALTITUDE: 1,180–4,080 feet (360–1,244m) above sea level.

LANDSCAPE: High, steep, and overhanging cliffs beside the Zambezi River as it flows from Mana Pools to Mupata Gorge in Chewore. The "pools" are natural channels ,"pinched" off from the river.

VEGETATION: Sparse forest and bush vegetation with mopane trees on the riverbanks. Savanna in the higher parts and in Chewore. On newer sandbanks close to the river an unusually dominant species of *Acacia albida*.

FAUNA: During the dry season game gathers along the riverbanks: elephants, lions, leopards, warthogs, zebras, cheetahs, African wild dogs, and antelopes such as greater kudus, elands, sable antelopes, and waterbucks. Chewore has black rhinoceroses. The river has lots of crocodiles and hippopotamuses. 380 bird species recorded; rich in fish.

CONSERVATION VALUE: The riverbank and "pools" are a haven for wildlife in the dry season.

TOURISM: Remote area with increasing level of visitors.

TSINGY BEMARAHA

—NEEDLE-SHARP ROCKS

The leaves of trees are a prized food among the sifakas, one of Madagascar's 35 species of lemur.

The jagged rocks in Petit Tsingy cover an area of nearly two-and-a-half acres (one hectare).

IN AMONG THE TREES STAND HOSTS OF upright rocks tightly packed together, resembling a petrified forest. The landscape is like nothing else we have seen and could be a man-made wonderland. We cannot get a good overview at all, because the tropical vegetation envelops the confusion of rocky spikes and hides it well.

We are in Petit Tsingy, the little stone forest, which lies on the edge of the Tsingy Bemaraha reserve in western Madagascar. Designated as early as 1927, this is the island's biggest nature conservation area. The word *tsingy* refers specifically to the remarkable rocks. There is a similar but smaller example on the northern side of the island.

We follow a path cleared through the swamp, climb up fixed ladders across the hard, gray, sometimes almost black, limestone and go down into narrow clefts, tens of feet deep, which form a labyrinthine maze. The rock pinnacles have jagged edges on which we easily graze ourselves. The slimmest of them sound hollow when we tap them.

The stone forest has been formed by chemical weathering. A large massif consisting of limestone constitutes the Bemaraha plateau, which in the east ends in a sudden precipice, but to the west slopes more gradually. Rainwater containing carbon dioxide eats away at the lime and, more or less, carves out each bare rock. Where the water runs straight down the mountainside, there are masses of parallel, hollowed-out grooves, making the mountain look like a sheet of corrugated iron. And the rocks have become sharpened, like arrowheads. Chemical weathering is not an unusual phenomenon in this area, with its calciferous rocks, but this startling result is without equal. A little farther north, inside the reserve, lies an even more outlandish area—Grand Tsingy—which has recently been opened to visitors. There, the rock pinnacles are even taller and wilder.

The Manambolo River forms the southern border of the conservation area. It has carved out a majestic and canyon-like river valley through which we are carried in wooden canoes to a place a few hundred feet below the limestone plateau. A man from the village nearby poles us against the current to a couple of caves in the surrounding rock walls, which are also the work of the carbon dioxide-rich water.

In the western, lowland part of the reserve there is a dry deciduous forest, containing many examples of the island's unique biology—for example, the strange baobab trees. Of the eight species, seven are found only on Madagascar. They are also called "bottle

The trunk of the rare giant baobab tree is a rock-hard column.

The word "tsingy" comes from the hollow ringing sound that you make when you stand on the rock.

Parson's chameleon is one of the biggest of all chameleon species.

trees" since they store water in their fat trunks—an adaptation to the largely rain-starved climate of this region. The animals most characteristic of Madagascar are the lemurs, but chameleons are not far behind as symbols of this country. All the species of lemur and half of all the chameleon species in the world are found only in Madagascar. In the forest around Bemaraha live four lemur species, including sportive lemurs and sifakas. There are many chameleons too—their colorful appearances constantly changing like a neverending, grotesque fashion show.

It is not for nothing that the world's fourth largest island is called "the land that time forgot." Madagascar broke away from Africa 160 million years ago, before the era of mammals—this is why it has no big game. The land became an island in the Indian Ocean and its wildlife evolved in its own, unique way. Of the 10,000 vascular plants found here, more than half are unique. The same can be said of the 256 bird species.

As early as 1771 Joseph Commerson wrote that Madagascar was "truly the snaturalist's promised land," and even today this is true, although it has been damaged since then. Large tracts of the island, such as Tsingy Bemaraha, remain little explored.

TSINGY BEMARAHA

REGISTERED: 1990.

COUNTRY: Madagascar.

FORM OF CONSERVATION: Nature reserve.

CRITERIA: Natural beauty, threatened species.

SIZE: 590 square miles (1,520sq km).

ALTITUDE: 490–2,300 feet (150–700m) above sea level.

LANDSCAPE: Large limestone plateau, which ends abruptly in the east with cliffs almost 1,300 feet (400m) high. The western side ends in slopes, with inaccessible formations of chemically weathered limestone in places. To the south the Manambolo River flows through a majestic canyon with caves.

VEGETATION: A dense dry and deciduous forest grows on the plateau. Several species of trees endemic to Madagascar. Succulents such as aloe vera among the rocks.

FAUNA: The reserve has a unique species of chameleon. 53 bird species, and 4 species of lemur, including the sifaka and the sportive lemur, have been recorded.

CULTURAL HISTORY: Western Madagascar is inhabited by the Sakalav people, who have a burial ground in the area.

CONSERVATION VALUE: Unique limestone rocks, and a large area of untouched and almost uninhabited country of great biological value.

TOURISM: 1,000 visitors per year.

ALDABRA
—A MAGICAL ATOLL

The red-footed booby nests among frigatebirds, even though the latter force them to regurgitate their food as they fly.

The Aldabra atoll is made up of old, raised coral reefs, as seen here framed by a casuarina tree in the foreground.

AN IMAGE OF OUTSTANDING ALDABRA TAKES SHAPE. A geological history of creation is played out on fast forward before our eyes. As our vessel approaches Aldabra, we see the 125,000-year-old atoll rise from the deep and push up through the horizon.

Imagine a small strip of land broken up into islands that surround a giant oval lagoon almost 20 miles (30km) long. It is a jagged collection of dead coral, inhabited by over 150,000 giant tortoises which are up to 150 years old, and weigh several hundred pounds. Above the atoll the clouds shimmer green by day and reddish-violet when the sun has set.

Aldabra is the world's largest raised atoll and one of the most isolated—a magical place. All day long it is the scene of an impressive tidal phenomenon. Huge volumes of water flow out of the lagoon with immense force, leaving it almost empty. No sooner have the waves exited when they start to come in again, through the narrow passageways.

For a long time passing sailors were deterred from going ashore on Aldabra by the tidal currents and the sharp reefs that had broken up many ships. If those who were shipwrecked managed to avoid the sharks and reach the shore, they then had to assuage their hunger with meat from the turtles and seabirds, and quench their thirst with rainwater and turtle urine, while they awaited rescue.

Our rubber dinghy rushes into the lagoon on the rising tide through Johnny Channel. An enormous green turtle swims unexpectedly quickly alongside us for a moment before it swerves like an airplane and disappears in the clear water. We slow down and chug gently toward a colony of frigatebirds and red-footed boobies. The former, with their 6-foot (2m) wingspans, hang like swarms of black sailplanes over the dense mangrove trees where they nest. With a population of 10,000 greater and lesser frigatebirds the Aldabra atoll is the Earth's second largest breeding ground for these two species. They are like pirates of the air, diving abruptly on the boobies to force them to regurgitate their catch. In spite of this daily battle the birds all nest in the same trees.

The turnstone, familiar to most European and North American birders as a non-breeder and wintering bird, lives up to its name, moving among the stones on the beach and turning them over at lightning speed. Less jerky in its movements is an Aldabra sacred ibis that comes strutting by along the sandy beach. It is white with

The reefs round Aldabra
were a source of delight for
Jacques-Yves Cousteau
in the 1950s, but in 1998
El Niño damaged a
large part of them.

These mushroom-shaped
coral islands, which have
been eroded by the
waves, are typical of
Aldabra's lagoon.

a black head—almost like its East African counterpart, but with eyes of a fragile pale blue, like the finest porcelain. The Aldabran drongo, with its forked tail, is unique to the island. The Comoro blue pigeon is blue, white, and red, and is called the *pigeon hollandais* after the Dutch flag. The Madagascar coucal darts up and down the tree trunks to surprise lizards, which lurk there.

Thanks to a few cat-free islands in the atoll, Aldabra's flightless, white-throated rails were spared the same fate as the dodo and the red rail on Mauritius, a solitaire on Réunion, another solitaire and Leguat's rail on Rodrigues, and the elephant bird on Madagascar. None of these birds could fly. Aldabra's rail is the last surviving flightless bird in the western Indian Ocean and therefore it greatly deserves protection. However, tragedy has already struck the Aldabran brush warbler whose fate is already sealed—the species was discovered as late as 1967 by a Royal Society expedition, but this timid brush warbler has not been seen since 1983, and is now deemed extinct.

During a snorkeling trip I see another green turtle floating by, its fins outstretched. It has a clumsy body, but in water it moves as easily as a bird in the sky. This threatened

species has a significant population on the Aldabra atoll. The beaches are thick with sand craters left by the turtles after their nightly egg laying.

But it is the giant tortoise, *Geochelone gigantea*, that is Aldabra's real hallmark. These armored, ancient creatures developed 180 million years ago on the primitive continent of Gondwanaland, before today's continents drifted apart. After Aldabra was raised above the sea's surface 125,000 years ago, they colonized the atoll. The animals heave themselves along over the open spaces on Picard, showing a predilection for the research station of the Seychelles Islands Foundation. They disport themselves in the water pools of Grande Terre when they need to cool down, and they manage to struggle through the brushwood forest and across the jagged, pocked banks of coral.

John Jourdain first wrote thus of the Seychelles' giant tortoises in his diary in 1609: "the boate brought soe many land tortells as they could well carrie," and they "were good meate, as good as fresh beef." In 1874 Charles Darwin wrote to the governor of Mauritius that "the rescue and protection of these animals is recommended, less on account of their utility … than on account of the great scientific interest." But

Giant tortoises roam close to the Seychelles Islands Foundation research station.

The Aldabra white-throated rail is the last flightless bird in the eastern Indian Ocean.

A greater frigatebird on an island in the lagoon. The young have white heads.

The land-dwelling robber crab has found a sanctuary on remote Aldabra.

the Mauritians were fully occupied with exterminating their own tortoises. From 1891 the atoll was leased by James Spurs, who immediately banned the hunting of tortoises. However, he also exploited the turtles, and introduced goats, which remain a nuisance to this day. The hunting ban led to a strong comeback by the giant tortoise, and in 2001 there was a population of about 152,000 animals.

Here in the coral reef the French film-maker Jacques-Yves Cousteau dived in the 1950s. In 1953 he applied—unsuccessfully—to lease Aldabra in order to protect the island. Since 1967, the scientist Professor David R. Stoddart has worked tirelessly to conserve Aldabra by studying the atoll and publishing his findings.

As late as the 1960s, the British wanted to build a military base and airfield on the island, but the world's scientists protested. After the Seychelles gained independence in 1976, the government proposed that Aldabra should be registered as a World Heritage site, which UNESCO did in 1982. But in spring 1998 a group of British researchers discovered raised temperatures in the surrounding sea and extensive color loss in the coral. Is this the new threat facing Aldabra?

ALDABRA

REGISTERED: 1982.

COUNTRY: Seychelles.

FORM OF CONSERVATION: Nature reserve.

CRITERIA: Ecology, natural beauty, threatened species.

SIZE: 135 square miles (350sq km), of which 72 square miles (188sq km) are land, and 8 square miles (20sq km) are mangrove thickets.

ALTITUDE: 0–26 feet (0–8m) above sea level.

LANDSCAPE: Oval atoll 21 by 9 miles (34 by 14.5km), comprising 4 oblong coral islands separated by narrow sounds. Shallow lagoon, 55 square miles (144sq km) with a 10-foot (3m) tide interval and wave-eroded islands. Well-developed coral reef.

VEGETATION: 178 species of vascular plants, 20% of which are unique, several threatened. Mangrove swamp frames the lagoon. Where the limestone is pitted, dense bush grows; on flat surfaces there are low trees, bushes, grass, and plants.

FAUNA: Unique, reptile-dominated animal life, with an extraordinary natural population of giant land tortoises, numbering 152,000. Green and hawksbill turtles lay eggs on the beaches. 13 species of terrestrial birds. Important nesting ground for red-tailed tropicbirds, greater and lesser frigatebirds, and red-footed boobies. 4 species of bat are the only native mammals. Important environment for robber crabs.

CONSERVATION VALUE: Large atoll on which have developed several different land forms and many endemic species. Tortoises, turtles, nesting seabirds, and the Aldabra white-throated rail.

TOURISM: Very few visitors, owing to the lack of regular transport.

VALLÉE DE MAI
—VALLEY OF THE COCO DE MER

A green gecko, seen here on the male inflorescence of the coco de mer palm.

A visit to the Vallée de Mai is a mysterious and primitive experience.

Following pages: The strange, twin-lobed fruit of the coco de mer, seen here lying on one of the tree's giant leaves, has given rise to many myths.

LIKE SHEETS OF CORRUGATED CARD, the enormous leaves of the coco de mer palm rub against one another above our heads. The Vallée de Mai on the Seychelles' second largest island, Praslin, is entirely dominated by palms, whose canopy blankets the floor of the forest in shadow. Our senses are all competing to absorb the inimitable atmosphere.

Long before the Seychelles were discovered, on rare occasions a mysterious giant nut with twin lobes floated ashore in India, Arabia, or on the Maldives. The rulers believed that the hard seed flesh increased their virility, and they decreed that keeping such a find secret could be punishable by death. The twin-lobed nut, weighing 33 pounds (15kg), is the biggest seed in the plant kingdom. It also seemed magical because of its appearance—the fruit is amazingly like a lifesize female pelvis. A legend arose that the fruit grew on a tree at the bottom of the sea. In 1768, when the French found the place where it grew in the Vallée de Mai, the species had already been given the name coco de mer, the "sea coconut", and the scientific name *Lodoicea maldivica*.

On a visit in 1881, the Victorian hero General Charles Gordon Pascha became absolutely convinced that he had found the remains of the Garden of Eden described in the Old Testament. For Gordon, the twin-lobed nut was the forbidden fruit and the palm was the tree of knowledge. He even found the serpent in his paradise— a harmless species of snake that lives in the forest. Gordon wrote of how the islands had been part of the land bridge between Asia and Madagascar, which together formed the continent of Lemuria. This was not such a crazy idea—thirty-five years before, Alfred Wegener came up with his continental drift theory. According to Wegener the Seychelles had belonged to the supercontinent Gondwanaland 250 million years ago and were left behind in the Indian Ocean when Africa, Madagascar, and India drifted apart. Since then the *Lodoicea* palm has evolved its present form in isolation.

There are many species which have found their own evolutionary routes out here in the Indian Ocean. The six species of palm in the valley are found nowhere else. The black silhouettes of flying foxes pass over the forest in the twilight. These huge bats came under their own steam across the sea from India and developed into a new species on the Seychelles. The green gecko came from Madagascar on rafts of driftwood. In the Vallée de Mai we see it sitting on the male inflorescence of the coco de mer tree. In the

The green tree frog is from Africa. It probably came to the Seychelles when the islands were still joined to the supercontinent of Gondwanaland.

A Seychelles sunbird visits a flower to feed on the nectar.

Originally from Asia, the flying fox has evolved into a new species during its isolation on the islands.

evening gloom river shrimp scuttle along the bottom of a stream in the light of our torches. Once, they walked up from the sea and adapted to fresh water.

Slugs and snails ooze up the green stems of the enormous sea coconut leaves, two of them unique to the Vallée de Mai. A chameleon, endemic to the Seychelles, swivels its protruding eyes and suddenly throws its sticky tongue at an unsuspecting insect. The green tree frog, which originated in Africa, blends in like a polished emerald in the equally green forest environment. A thin whistle is heard from above the forest canopy. The Seychelles black parrot—*cateau noir*—which is also unique to the Vallée de Mai, was shot by plantation owners in the nineteenth century. By 1965 only fifty were left.

The Vallée de Mai is easily accessible to visitors. But caution is advisable when dusk falls. According to folklore, at night the yard-long inflorescence of the male tree rises up and seeks the female "haunches" of the double coconut, and anyone who witnesses this encounter is doomed to die a violent death. Apart from such "protection," all the species in the forest enjoy respect today thanks to the valley's twofold conservation status as both a national park and a World Heritage site.

VALLÉE DE MAI

REGISTERED: 1983.

COUNTRY: Seychelles.

FORM OF CONSERVATION:
National park.

CRITERIA: Geology, ecology,
natural beauty, and threatened
species.

SIZE: 50 acres (0.2sq km).

ALTITUDE: 525–655 feet
(160–200m) above sea level.

LANDSCAPE: Mountain valley
on the island of Praslin.
3 streams rise here and flow
out to sea on different sides
of the island.

VEGETATION: The valley is covered
with a 100–130-foot (30–40m)
high palm forest, dominated
by the unique coco de mer tree,
Lodoicea maldivica, the
Seychelles native palm species
and the fan-like *Pandanus*.
Also unique deciduous trees
of the genera *Northea*,
Drypetes, and *Dillenia*.

FAUNA: Island species. Unique
subspecies of black parrot,
which lives in the palm forest.
Other endemic birds are
Seychelles sunbirds, blue

pigeons, and Seychelles
kestrels. The only endemic
mammals are the flying fox and
the Seychelles sheath-tailed
bat. 1 native chameleon, several
species of gecko, 2 of snakes.
In the streams, the islands'
only endemic fish species.

CONSERVATION VALUE: Wide range
of flora and fauna, the only
area with all the Seychelles'
palms, and the unique coco
de mer tree.

TOURISM: Financed by entrance
fee and sale of cocos de mer.

ASIA

Asia is the world's biggest continent, encompassing many extreme natural phenomena: the Himalayas is the Earth's highest mountain chain and Siberia's taiga has the most extensive coniferous forests; in southeast Asia we find the oldest rainforests, and in Tibet the largest high plateau in the world; while the Russian Federation has lakes that are large enough to be called seas. Most of the sites in Asia have acquired World Heritage status because of their beauty or the incidence of threatened species, while a few have been chosen for their ecology or geology. The region also has six combined natural and cultural sites. We were able to experience small areas of this massive continent when we were surrounded by birds in Keoladeo Ghana; encountered tigers and rhinoceroses while riding elephants in Chitwan and Kaziranga; walked among Sagarmatha's colossal massifs; and shot the rapids in the rivers of the Altai Mountains.

CHITWAN

—HEART OF THE JUNGLE

Riding an elephant is a bone-shaking experience, but it is the best way to get around in the jungle.

During the dry season the Rapti River is a mere trickle in the savanna, beneath the rounded foothills of the Himalayas.

IT IS AFTERNOON IN THE JUNGLE, a soft filtered sunlight peeps in between the treetops and encounters the yard-high panicles of grass, which glow a gilded yellow. Nature lies silent like an empty church. There is no wind and the heat shimmers. The elephant on which we are sitting ambles along gently and the mahout taps it lightly with his bare feet to get it to stop. Tiger tracks are visible around the remains of a slain chital and our hopes are raised, but after a while the elephant continues, plowing its way through the dense vegetation. We do not see any striped big cats, but merely breathing in the highly charged atmosphere when a tiger is around in the jungle is no mean experience.

Chitwan—the word probably means "the heart of the jungle"—is a haven for tigers, but they are difficult to see. The national park is equally famous for its Indian rhinoceroses and a third of the world population of these animals is found here. Like many other national parks on the Indian subcontinent, the area was formerly a hunting reserve, created in the nineteenth century by the Rana dynasty, which ruled Nepal until 1950. Huge numbers of animals were senselessly shot, but the hunting had one benefit—the jungle was protected from settlement and cultivation. Another deterrent to humans was malaria. When the Rana family lost its power, the hunting ceased and at the same time the risk of malaria was reduced as a result of intensive DDT insecticide spraying. Chitwan was then invaded by settlers, and the new leaders of Nepal feared that wild game would disappear from the area, so they created a nature reserve and forced the 22,000 human inhabitants to leave their homes. Later, the reserve was converted into a national park, and Chitwan is now considered one of the best kept in Asia. Wild elephants from the adjacent Parsa Game Reserve pass through the park regularly. The number of rhinoceroses and tigers has grown since the 1970s, but the tigers are once again under threat from poachers.

During an elephant ride through leafy glades we first see several different species of deer, and then a female Indian rhinoceros with her calf. As we approach them we are no longer alone—about ten more elephants with passengers quickly crowd around the rhinoceros. Seeing the Earth's fourth biggest land animal is an experience to fire the imagination, but at the same time the situation leaves an uncomfortable impression. There we are sitting safely on our elephants, observing two ancient creatures who face

A liana, a type of woody vine, slowly strangles its victim, which is a tree in the jungle.

The chital is common in Chitwan. This beautiful deer emits a shrill warning call when threatened by a tiger.

the same intrusion day after day. The animals are noticeably irritated—they can have no conception that tourism is necessary to preserve their environment.

The people around Chitwan want to utilize the area. The tall grass can be used for constructing houses and the jungle cleared for planting. The park administrators now allow the villagers to cut down the grass along the rivers at the beginning of every year. This makes the game easier to find and encourages healthy, new vegetation to grow, providing excellent grazing for the rhinoceroses and deer.

Tourism provides employment, but in the north, where all the hotels are situated, the jungle has become criss-crossed with elephant trails. The management of Chitwan now feels that the area cannot take any more visitors. Although only a limited part of the park is being exploited, the other areas are to remain untouched. This is a typical example of the difficulty in balancing conservation and tourism in places that are rich in wildlife. It is thanks to the many visitors that the national park is accepted and that nature can be preserved and the animals survive. The price is a certain amount of wear and tear and disruption, but on the whole Chitwan is a very well-preserved jungle.

CHITWAN

REGISTERED: 1984.

COUNTRY: Nepal.

FORM OF CONSERVATION: National park.

CRITERIA: Ecology, natural beauty, threatened species.

SIZE: 360 square miles (932sq km).

ALTITUDE: 490–2,675 feet (150–815m) above sea level.

LANDSCAPE: Between two river valleys lies a mountain ridge covered in jungle. Along the rivers, the savanna-like grasslands flood regularly.

VEGETATION: Floods, fires, and erosion have created a mosaic of grasslands and different types of forest. The jungle of sal trees (*Shorea robusta*) covers more than 60% of the area. Open ground with elephant grass accounts for around 20% of the land area.

FAUNA: Populations of around 450 Indian rhinoceroses and 50 tigers. Leopards, Indian wild dogs, and sloth bears have stable populations. Wild elephants pass through regularly. Gavials and river dolphins are found in the waterways. 490 bird species observed.

CULTURAL HISTORY: The Tharu people have inhabited the surrounding area for centuries.

CONSERVATION VALUE: The best preserved jungle in southern Nepal and an important area for the survival of Indian rhinoceroses, gavials, and tigers.

TOURISM: 100,000 visitors per year.

KAZIRANGA

—HOME OF THE RHINOCEROS

JUST AS WE CLIMB ONTO THE ELEPHANT'S BACK in Mihimukh the sun rises over the hills. In Assam's Kaziranga National Park four-legged travel works best through the tall *nal* or elephant grass, and the wet marshes. The experience is also more authentic on the back of an Asian elephant, because these animals have lived here for thousands of years.

Wild buffaloes wallow in Kaziranga's small lakes, and out on the grasslands we are watched by swamp deer—barasinghas. We disappear into the 20-feet (6m) high grass, which can hide tigers, rhinoceroses, and armed poachers. Suddenly, a mighty Indian rhinoceros is staring at us. Its skin is like armor plating, fixed to its body with iron bolts—a two-ton tank with prehistoric features. Rhinoceros horn commands a high price as an aphrodisiac in the Far East, a factor that has brought the species to the brink of extinction. Although about thirty rhinoceroses have been killed every year inside the park, approximately 1,250 live on there. The armed guards also help protect the tigers, whose numbers have increased from twenty to eighty since 1986. The heavy seasonal floods take their toll. For example, in 1998 forty-two rhinos and 610 other large animals perished in the monsoon rains. However, despite such setbacks, the future of the rhinoceros looks brighter today. Kaziranga has won a prestigious prize from the WWF for courageous work in difficult circumstances, without much support from the state.

Barasingha, or swamp deer, move around in small herds while they graze on the wide grasslands.

The Indian rhinoceros is a threatened species, much sought after by poachers, but it is surviving relatively well today in Kaziranga.

KAZIRANGA

REGISTERED: 1985.
COUNTRY: India (Assam).
FORM OF CONSERVATION: National park.
CRITERIA: Ecology, threatened species.
SIZE: 166 square miles (430sq km).
ALTITUDE: 130–260 feet (40–80m) above sea level.
LANDSCAPE: Flood plain along the Brahmaputra River. Grasslands, open forests, and many small lakes, or "bheels." 75% of the area is submerged when it floods.
VEGETATION: 20-foot (6m) high elephant grass on the higher land to the west. Smaller species of grass on the lowlands around the lakes. Grasses affected by fires and floods. Grass covers more than half the area, open tropical jungle a third.
FAUNA: 15 threatened species of mammal. 1,250 animals or 60% of the world's Indian rhinoceros population, and almost as many wild Asian elephants. Tigers, leopards, sloth bears. Ungulates such as gaurs, sambars, and barasinghas. Around 300 bird species, of which 100 are migratory.
CONSERVATION VALUE: One of southern Asia's best wildlife areas with many threatened species, including Indian rhinoceroses and tigers.
TOURISM: 20,000 visitors per year, mostly Indian. Political unrest has reduced tourism.

KEOLADEO GHANA
—THE WETLANDS OF BIRDS

The little egret heron is
a common species in
the Ghana marshlands.

A white-breasted kingfisher
watches over the marsh,
which is still flooded in
November, long after
the monsoon rains.

Following pages: Indian
shags sit in a dead tree,
sihouetted against the sun
as it sets over the bush.

WE CYCLE AT A LEISURELY PACE through a tunnel of leaves while rhesus monkeys sit beside the road, staring pensively. To right and left the wetlands glint behind galleries of trees, teeming with birdlife. The road leads to a place that is popular at sunset. Against the background of a fiery sky sit several cormorants, silhouetted in the skeleton of a dead tree. Darkness falls equatorially fast, at the same time as a highly charged silence descends on the previously frantic wildlife.

The Keoladeo Ghana National Park in India is relatively small and isolated from its densely populated surroundings. The park is man-made and well visited, but all the birds and the game come here by natural routes. Keoladeo Ghana is a marsh that originally consisted of bush savanna. Maharajah Harbmaji, who owned the land at the end of the nineteenth century, saw the possibility of creating a special hunting area and he had the savanna flooded in 1899. The result exceeded all expectations. The ponds and the marshlands that were created attracted enormous numbers of seabirds. The maharajah's hunting project had given India one of the world's best sanctuaries for birds. Although hunting accounted for the slaughter of large quantities of birds—the daily record was over 4,000 birds—ducks and waders returned in undiminished numbers. Much later, in 1956, the area was given protection as a bird sanctuary, but hunting continued for almost another ten years. When it finally stopped, other problems arose. The neighboring villagers let their cattle graze on the fertile land and tourism caused disruption. To control the situation the area was upgraded to a national park in 1982.

The wetlands are also known as Bharatpur, after a nearby town. Keoladeo is a name derived from that of the old Shiva temple inside the park, but locally the area is simply called Ghana, which means "dense" and refers to the vegetation. The open marshes are surrounded by brush and the whole area is a rich mosaic of wildlife. The southern parts of the national park consist of bush savanna. There, we see big herds of sambar and nilgai grazing on grass that is still green, even in November, a couple of months after the monsoon season. In July, when the rains come, the marsh quickly soaks up the water, which is brought here from two rivers through a system of dams. The water is let out through a series of canals. Small lakes form, which contain a hotchpotch of fish, leeches, algae, beetles, and frogs that attract thousands of seabirds and waders to feed and

Five species of kingfisher inhabit the park, including this white-breasted kingfisher.

The Indian pond heron likes catching frogs and lizards.

An Indian python winds its way up into a tree.

The Indian darter eats fish, which it harpoons with its bill.

nest there. Around 120 bird species nest in Ghana, including eleven different kinds of heron. The heron colonies are believed to be the biggest in the world.

The purpose-built cycle tracks enable us to go right in among the birds. Around 150,000 birds from northern climes winter here. Including visitors, over 360 species have been observed—a world record for such a small area. Four species of crane are seen regularly. Previously, a large proportion of the entire population of Siberian white cranes—150 pairs—wintered here, but now only a few birds are seen each year.

In rowing boats the villagers work to clear water hyacinths, which are spreading like weeds across the surface of the water. In some places we are so close to the birds that we do not even need binoculars to determine the species. Sometimes birds of prey and vultures sail on the thermal currents overhead. Thirteen species of eagle have been observed and four different species of vulture. We have an exciting encounter with an Indian python that has slithered up into a tree. This snake usually lurks in porcupine holes, to the mutual benefit of them both, and it is often seen in Keoladeo Ghana, which is not just a bird paradise, but also a haven for other wildlife.

KEOLADEO GHANA

REGISTERED: 1985.

COUNTRY: India (Rajasthan).

FORM OF CONSERVATION: National park.

CRITERIA: Threatened species.

SIZE: 11 square miles (29sq km).

ALTITUDE: 571 feet (174m) above sea level.

LANDSCAPE: Marshland on the Ganges plain with dammed wetlands mixed with forests and bush. There are ponds, marsh, canals, dikes, and sluices. During the monsoon large areas are covered with 3–6 feet (1–2m) of water, which recedes after the rains. The remainder of the area measures just half the size of the flooded area.

VEGETATION: On the solid ground deciduous forests grow, dominated by the Indian kadam, jamun, and babul trees. Where the trees have been felled there are large grass plains and scrublands.

FAUNA: Over 360 bird species observed. It is estimated that 12,000 storks, herons, and cormorants nest here, while 150,000 different ducks spend the winter, as does the extremely rare Siberian white crane. Rhesus monkeys and langurs are common. Small predators, such as the striped hyena and jackal seen occasionally. Several species of ungulates: nilgai, blackbucks, axis, and sambars. Large numbers of Indian python.

CONSERVATION VALUE: One of the world's best locations for birds and one of the most important overwintering sites for waterbirds from all over Asia, including several threatened species.

TOURISM: 100,000 visitors per year.

SAGARMATHA

—THE WORLD'S HIGHEST MOUNTAIN

Hybrids of yaks and cattle
make invaluable beasts
of burden.

Twilight over Nuptse,
25,870 feet (7,885m) high.

Following pages: From this
perspective snowclad
Nuptse appears higher than
black Mount Everest.

THE KALA PATTAR MOUNTAIN CREST, at 18,135 feet (5,500m) high, is just a paltry little bump in the Himalayas. All around it rise much higher peaks, each more rugged than the next. Yet it is Mount Everest, 6 miles (10km) away, that catches our attention, with its mainly black peak. In terms of altitude, it is another 10,000 feet (3,000m) higher—an elevation that is almost beyond comprehension.

The world's highest mountain exudes a magic like few other places in nature. Seeing the peak from Kala Pattar makes us both exultant and thoughtful. In 1923 George Leigh Mallory answered the question why he wanted to climb Mount Everest, with the mysterious reply, "Because it's there." Now we know what he meant. After all, it is not a particularly beautiful peak, its daunting solidity often hidden behind the other giant mountains. In 1848 a group of surveyors saw Mount Everest from a distance, and after four years of calculations they concluded that it was the highest mountain of all.

The name given to it honored the retired and respected head of the Survey of India office, Sir George Everest. However, the Tibetans and Sherpas had their own name for it—Chomolungma—which in the Tibetan language means "mother goddess of the world." This name is still used, but during the 1970s the authorities in Nepal launched a new name—Sagarmatha—which is Sanskrit and means "goddess of the sky." In spite of this, Mount Everest is the still the mountain's most widely used name.

The first calculations gave its height as 29,002 feet (8,840m), a figure that stood until the 1950s when an Indian study revealed that the mean value measured from several vantage points was 29,028 feet (8,848m). A scientific expedition recently measured the mountain using accurate satellite methods and found the height to be 29,035 feet (8,850m), but even this figure will need to be revised in the future, as Everest grows 1–1.5 inches (3–4cm) higher each year.

In the 1920s the first attempts were made to climb Everest from the Tibetan side. During the 1924 expedition George Mallory and Andrew Irvine disappeared below the peak, but the question of whether they reached the top has never been answered. Seventy-five years later Mallory's remains were found high up on the north face. In the 1930s new attempts to climb the mountain were made from the north, but when Nepal first opened its doors to the outside world in 1950, the unknown south face attracted

A sacred inscription on a
stone under Mount Taboche.
Sherpas practice the Tibetan
form of Buddhism.

A Sherpa girl with her child.
Many of the young people
work in the tourist industry.

The bridge over Dudh Kosi is
one of several suspension
bridges on the way
to Mount Everest.

more interest. It was the great British expedition of 1953 that was crowned with success, when on May 29 a New Zealander, Edmund Hillary, and a Sherpa, Tensing Norgay, finally stood on the roof of the world.

The area south of Everest is the Sherpas' homeland. These people came here from eastern Tibet during the sixteenth century, and lived by trading across the high mountain passes. Today many make their living from tourism. During the 1970s the number of expeditions and treks caused large quantities of wood to be consumed, litter increased and waste disposal became a serious issue. The Sagarmatha National Park was then born at Edmund Hillary's instigation. Initially, the Sherpas were against the establishment of a park because it meant that they were no longer allowed to cultivate new land, fell trees, or keep goats. Now they are extremely positive about it, not least because the landscape has recovered well. However, perhaps in the future the number of visitors will have to be limited because the area is attracting more and more tourists. The reasons why are simple—there are three mountains over 26,250 feet (8,000m) high and all the dimensions in this outstanding and magnificent national park are extreme.

SAGARMATHA

REGISTERED: 1979.

COUNTRY: Nepal.

FORM OF CONSERVATION:
National park.

CRITERIA: Natural beauty.

SIZE: 443 square miles
(1,148sq km).

ALTITUDE: 9,330–29,035 feet
(2,845–8,850m) above
sea level.

LANDSCAPE: Dramatic mountains,
still rising in altitude. The rivers
were there before the latest
major folding 500,000 years
ago. The main river, Bhote Kosi,
is born out of huge glaciers and
runs through a deeply incised
valley. 3 peaks over 26,250 feet
(8,000m) and 7 over 22,965 feet
(7,000m).

VEGETATION: Three quarters of the
surface is barren rock, snow,
and ice. Below the steep peaks
there are meadows and heaths.
In the river valleys coniferous
forests grow up to 9,840 feet
(3,000m) above sea level. Above
that, rhododendrons and birch
forest. Treeline is between
12,465 and 13,125 feet
(3,800–4,000m) above sea level.
Alpine *Gentiana*, *Primula*, and
Potentilla are common.

FAUNA: Only small populations
of wild animals owing to
human presence. Himalayan
thar and musk deer now more
common. Snow leopards seen
regularly. 152 bird species
found, such as lammergeiers,
Tibetan snowcocks, and
blood pheasants.

CULTURAL HISTORY: 3,500 resident
Sherpas. Several villages and
Buddhist monasteries. Cattle
sheds in the main valleys, at
high altitudes.

CONSERVATION VALUE: Landscape
of outstanding beauty. One of
the most interesting areas in the
world geologically. Valuable for
the biology of the Himalayas
and the culture of the Sherpas.

TOURISM: 25,000 visitors per year.

NANDA DEVI

—THE FORBIDDEN PEAK

The Himalayan thar is common in the national park.

Hindus regard Nanda Devi as "the goddess of happiness," and the inhabitants of the mountains sacrifice buffaloes and goats in her honor. Here the peak is seen from the west.

INDIA'S HIGHEST MOUNTAIN beckons, an unattainable temptation 19 miles (30km) away. We see it from the path along a steep valley side and we cannot approach any closer than this. The rugged peak rises all alone above a wall of snowclad rock faces that enclose the Nanda Devi National Park—the most untouched and forbidden area in the Himalayas. Its only opening into the outside world is the deep Rashi Ganga ravine, and for the last fifteen years nobody has been allowed to enter there. A great feeling of reverence envelops us as we see the protected peak in the distance.

As recently as 1934 a few people managed to enter the area, including the Britons Eric Shipton and H. W. Tilman. Two years later Tilman climbed Nanda Devi with an American, Noel Odell. In 1939 when the Indian authorities learned of this incursion into hitherto untouched territory, a reserve was established, with strict rules governing access. In 1974 the area was opened up for expeditions, and ten years later, it was designated a national park. By that time climbers and trekkers had begun to erode the land and a ban on visitors was reintroduced. Through strict protection the park is a last bastion of "uncivilization." It offers a haven to many of the Himalayas' threatened animals, among them snow leopards, and bharas, which in evolutionary terms are intermediate between goats and sheep—here they can live undisturbed.

NANDA DEVI

REGISTERED: **1988.**
COUNTRY: **India.**
FORM OF CONSERVATION: **National park.**
CRITERIA: **Natural beauty, threatened species.**
SIZE: **243 square miles (630sq km).**
ALTITUDE: **6,890–25,645 feet (2,100–7,817m) above sea level.**
LANDSCAPE: **A glacial and high alpine landscape with steep fells. Nanda Devi is India's highest peak and the 30th highest mountain in the world.**

VEGETATION: **Fir forest of the genus** *Abies* **grows in the lower parts. Farther up the mountain there is rhododendron and birch forest up to 10,990 feet (3,350m). Above the treeline there are meadows with juniper bushes. Almost 630 species of vascular plants.**
FAUNA: **14 different mammals recorded. Predators, such as snow leopards, leopards, and Asian black bears are found. 80 bird species.**

CULTURAL HISTORY: **The protected area around the mountain has always been uninhabited, owing to its inaccessibility.**
CONSERVATION VALUE: **One of the most untouched and desolate areas in the Himalayas. High incidence of species whose existence is threatened elsewhere.**
TOURISM: **The national park is closed to both local mountain people and tourists.**

ALTAI MOUNTAINS
—THE GOLDEN CHAIN

A family in the village of Aktasj in the inner Altai region greets the helicopter pilot when he arrives with the mail.

The Altai Mountains display different characteristics from the inner region. Here, green sparsely forested ridges succeed one another as far as the eye can see.

THE PATH TEETERS HIGH UP ON THE CREST of a steep slope—grassy but bereft of trees. In the V-shaped valley bottom a stream flows rapidly along to meet the Kadrin River lower down. The maral deer answer from the other side of the valley when Nikolaj, a local hunter in a lynx fur cap, imitates their grunts with his horn. We find droppings from maral and wolves on the path, the bones from a deer the wolves have killed, and down in the brush zone several daytime lairs of deer.

The next morning, when we are not disturbing the hunting of the Altai people, they catch two deer and a bear. The deer antlers and genitals are hung on separate forked sticks in accordance with ancient tradition. The meat is dried on the washing line and for the next several days we eat bear and venison roasted over an open camp fire and boiled in rich game stews. With the food we drink tea—*chai*—prepared from small, dried, maple-like leaves that Nikolaj has gathered from bushes on the edge of the forest.

The camp stands in a magnificent setting by a small stream, surrounded by extensive virgin forests of taiga spruce, and decorated with splashes of birch in its golden, fall colors. This is a beautiful, mountainous, south Siberian landscape randomly painted in red and yellow. Beyond the nearest hills rise barren gray peaks reminiscent of the Rocky Mountains, with crowns capped in snow.

We build a primitive sauna where the stream meets the Kadrin River. Sacha, Vladimir, and Natasja pile up round stones, under which they burn a fire. A big tarpaulin is spread over a few birch branches that have been arched over the stone "stove." The sauna is ready. Inside we throw river water on the hot stones and beat each other with birch twigs while the hot steam envelops our bodies—a touch bizarre but it would be hard to find a nicer sauna. When we cannot stand the heat any longer we throw ourselves into the cold, fall river.

Wildlife tourism is beginning to develop in the Altai Mountains, perhaps a contribution to the future conservation of this virgin wilderness. On our way back to civilization we ride rubber rafts over the rapids, we set up camp again on the shore of the Katun River, we build a new alfresco sauna, we walk over the mountains, and finally we are picked up by a Russian Army helicopter. The pilot takes us to Teletskoye—the deepest lake in Siberia after Lake Baikal, with a depth of 1,065 feet (325m).

We fly close to Belukha, the highest massif in the "Golden Mountains of Altai," as this breathtaking region on the border between Siberia, Mongolia, and China is called. These mineral-rich tracts conceal gold, silver, and copper. The mountain chain was first formed when the sediment of the old sea bottom folded 150 million years ago.

We trek through several climate and vegetation zones in the mountains, and observe a great number of plant species. More than a tenth of them are found nowhere else. The snow leopard is one of the Altai's thirteen red-listed animal species. The region is also significant for its hydrological balance, because one of Asia's biggest river systems, the Ob and Irtysh, rises in the Altai, where there are thousands of square miles of glaciers.

In the region there are traces of humans dating back a million years. Graves of tribal leaders 2,500 years old and other prehistoric remains of the Scythians have been found. A small number of herders live in the World Heritage site, making a living from grazing sheep and cattle. Enormous areas are still uninhabited and subject to strict conservation, with a human presence limited. Altai is one of the most untouched mountain chains on Earth and an area worthy of conservation.

ALTAI MOUNTAINS

REGISTERED: 1998.

COUNTRY: Altai Republic (Russian Federation).

FORM OF CONSERVATION: 3 nature reserves, 1 natural monument, 1 species and biotope reserve.

CRITERIA: Geology, ecology, natural beauty, threatened species.

SIZE: 6,220 square miles (16,115sq km).

ALTITUDE: 360–14,785 feet (109–4,506m) above sea level.

LANDSCAPE: The Altai Mountains have high peaks, 1500 glaciers, and provide the source of the Ob and Irtysh rivers. Almost 1,300 lakes, including the clear, 1,065-feet (325m) deep Lake Teletskoye. VEGETATION: Forests with larch, Siberian silver fir, and Siberian stone pine, mixed with aspen. The treeline lies at 5,900–6,230 feet (1,800–1,900m). Tree-covered steppes below the forests. 2,000 species of plants of which 200 are endemic. Above the coniferous forest, subalpine forests with rhododendron, cedar, and deciduous trees. Alpine meadows.

FAUNA: 60 mammals, such as pikas (tailess rabbit-like animals), arctic ground squirrels, sables, marals, and reindeer. Threatened species, such as the snow leopard and Mongolian gazelle. 300 bird species, including golden and imperial eagles and gyr falcons. 11 species of reptiles and amphibians.

CULTURAL HISTORY: Around 100 burial mounds with relics dating from the 6th century BCE, as well as many older, prehistoric remains.

CONSERVATION VALUE: Considerable biological diversity for northern Asia. Many threatened species.

TOURISM: Sparse but increasing. Large parts are prohibited to all except researchers.

OCEANIA

Oceania is the collective term for Australia, New Zealand, and most of the islands in the Pacific. Australia is a continent in itself, consisting mainly of desert and dry brushwood steppes. In the north and east, tree savanna and deciduous forest take over until the land along the east coast rises into a long mountain chain with rainforest. Many countries in the Pacific, from New Zealand to Hawaii, have steep mountains and volcanoes, while the rest of this island world consists of coral isles. Oceania's natural heritage sites have mainly been chosen for their ecological and esthetic value; most of Australia's sites have been registered because of their unique geology and threatened species. In Kakadu and Uluru–Kata Tjuta we encountered an Aborigine culture 40,000 years old; on the Great Barrier Reef, the rich diversity of the coral reef; in the Wet Tropics, the remnants of a rainforest; in New Zealand, fiord landscapes; and in Hawaii, volcanoes.

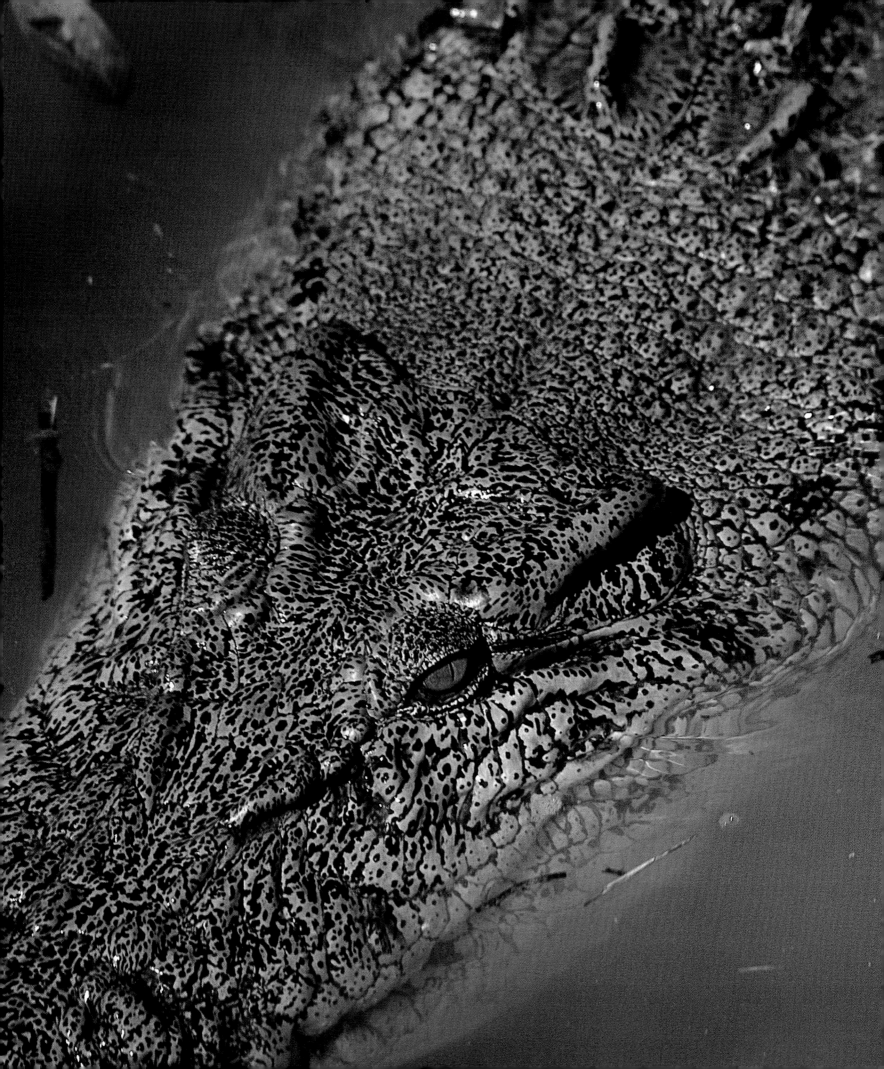

KAKADU

—INSPIRATIONAL COUNTRY

The kookaburra or laughing jackass is a big kingfisher that lives mostly on land-based vertebrates.

Thousands of years ago, the Aborigines sought shelter in the caves of Kakadu.

Following pages: Kakadu's landscape changes rapidly from grassy plains with wetlands and forest to steep sandstone rocks and fault lines.

THE TWILIGHT FALLS LIKE BLACK SILK over Darwin in northern Australia. After appreciating Aboriginal art in the town's museum, we set out into the bush, where these indigenous people have lived for at least 50,000 years. In the Northern Territory there are more Aborigines than anywhere else in Australia—a quarter of the inhabitants are black, speak a total of forty Aboriginal languages, and own half the land.

A beautiful map opens out beneath us as the little Cessna aircraft drones in over the flat country of the north coast and the Kakadu National Park. The bush is a mosaic of sparse, deciduous forest with grass and bush undergrowth, islands of rock, and streams, rivers, and waterholes or *billabongs*. The thigh-high grass scrapes itchy marks on our legs and hooks its seeds onto our socks. An airy forest of paperbark trees is part of the wilderness of northern Australia. On the sheets of flaking bark the Aborigines have painted their traditional patterns and mythical figures for thousands of years.

The multitude of wildlife in Kakadu is also apparent in the form of extensive wetlands: everything from tidal banks and mangrove swamps by the sea to enclosed marshes with lotus flowers in the south. The branches of a major river system all lie within the park boundaries and waterfalls tumble over a 985-feet (300m) high sandstone escarpment during the rainy season.

One morning we glide along in a flat-bottomed boat on South Alligator River. Two majestic white-bellied sea eagles rise from a treetop by the river; glossy ibis, with their curved bills, are silhouetted against the sky. There is a whistling in the air from a flock of ducks rising on their propeller wings over the water lilies in a marsh, while a jabiru stork lumberingly gains height with its heavy 6-feet (2m) wingspan. The visitor is struck by the enormous wealth of birdlife in Kakadu. Two to three million water birds flood the park between August and October. In a clearing among the trees a few flying foxes land upside down like trapeze artists in black jackets—they play an important part in the pollination of trees, including the eucalyptus and paperbark.

We visit rocky overhangs and caves where the Aborigines painted their Dreamtime. In Kakadu alone there are more than 7,000 sites with cave paintings, of which half have been registered by the park administrators. The pigment used was ocher, which gives strong colors when finely ground and heated, and provides a particularly powerful red.

Nancy, an Aborigine, weaves a bag from plant fibers in Kakadu.

There are thousands of cave paintings in Kakadu and Arnhem Land, some of them 40,000 years old.

One of the great variety of parrots found in Australia.

Termite mounds are common in Kakadu, on the grasslands and in the sparse forests.

A new world opens up in these caves, a dizzying universe of Aboriginal myths and history. The domed ceilings of the caves display shoals of baramundi, saratoga, crocodiles, wallabies, rainbow serpents, tortoises, birds, luma-luma, yawk-yawk, and a number of other beings from the Aboriginal creative tradition. In the Dreamtime the primeval mother Warramurrungundj sent out her creative beings to fill the continent with forest, rocks, pools, rivers, flowers, animals, birds, and finally also with *binninj*—humans. The "songlines" along which the forefathers walked and "sang life into the landscape" cross Australia invisibly and pass many sacred places. We experience the honor of seeing this prehistoric and expressive art, its sensitivity having lost nothing through the centuries.

The Earth's indigenous peoples can teach us an infinite amount about nature and the value of conserving it better. The faiths of such peoples are almost always tied to protective forces of nature, while the role of their ancestors reveals a deeply rooted respect for nature. Rituals honor both the ancestors and the mythical figures who have contributed to such a priceless fabric, and one of the best places to gain a better insight is the world heritage of Kakadu in northern Australia.

KAKADU

REGISTERED: 1981, extended 1987, 1992.

COUNTRY: Australia (Northern Territory).

FORM OF CONSERVATION: National park.

CRITERIA: Geology, ecology, natural beauty, threatened species.

SIZE: 7,650 square miles (19,804sq km).

ALTITUDE: 0–1,705 feet (0–520m) above sea level.

LANDSCAPE: Arnhem Land rises to the east in a 985-feet (300m) high, steep escarpment. Its sandstone rocks have developed isolated outcrops, caves, and clefts. The lowland in the west is surrounded by a flat flood plain, drained by the river system.

VEGETATION: Monsoon forest with eucalyptus, and tall grass that is burned regularly. Along the coast tidal marshes alternate with mangrove swamps. Rivers are bordered by grassy plains and broad wetlands that flood in the rainy season. More than 1,600 vascular plants. Many endemic species.

FAUNA: 64 species of mammals, such as kangaroos, dingoes, and dugongs. Water buffaloes and wild boar introduced. Estuarine crocodiles, freshwater crocodiles, and goannas. 39 species of snakes. A third of Australia's total bird species found here; 274 species recorded. Large numbers of water and shorebirds.

CULTURAL HISTORY: Thousands of Aboriginal cave paintings. More than 1,000 sites excavated.

CONSERVATION VALUE: Comprises the whole precipitation area for a monsoon-related tropical river. Outstandingly rich animal and plant life; unique cave paintings.

TOURISM: 300,000 visitors per year, rising sharply.

ULURU–KATA TJUTA

—THE SACRED DESERT ROCKS

A chain has been fixed on the rock to help climbers.

The rock's Aborigine guardians would prefer that no one ascend Uluru, but they accept that the climb is a major tourist attraction.

EVEN FROM A DISTANCE the silhouette of Uluru stands out. This 1,150-feet (350m) high rock rises abruptly from Australia's flat desert—and because we have become used to seeing an endless horizon it seems inexplicably out of place. When we look at this projection at close quarters the effect is so striking that we can scarcely believe our eyes. Is it a mirage, a giant massif, or a mammoth sculpture? Uluru is one of the world's mightiest monoliths and a geological riddle. Equally mysterious is Kata Tjuta, 19 miles (30km) to the west, a closely connected group of rock domes and outcrops. Why are these two landmarks here, quite alone, like desert islands in a sea?

Both these massifs have their origin 600 million years ago, when material from a broken-down mountain chain was carried here by running water. At Kata Tjuta an assorted mass containing both boulders and fine-grained sediment was dumped, while the more homogeneous sand was carried to Uluru. Millions of years later these deposits were flooded by the ocean. The pressure from the sea bottom cemented them into hard rocks: at Kata Tjuta a conglomerate was formed, and at Uluru a coarse-grained sandstone. After another couple of hundred million years the whole area was raised when a new mountain chain folded farther to the north. The Earth's movements tilted the sandstone at Uluru vertical, while the strata in Kata Tjuta were laid down at an angle. Then there was a long period of erosion. They are still being pushed gently upward and, just like an iceberg, they are much bigger under the surface.

The weathering at Uluru is intensive. The rocks split into huge slabs as a result of temperature changes. Heaps of loosened boulders are stacked at the base of the rocks. Wind and rain abrade the surface, which is gradually being perforated with chemically hollowed pits and holes. The whole mass looks like a giant, knobbly muffin with parallel bars across it. During the day it appears to change color, from cinnamon at noon to rust red in the twilight. After pouring rain the rock is as gray as ash and as slippery as soap.

Kata Tjuta has a different character, more like an archipelago on land, with steep outcrops close together. The six largest are huge and the highest stands 1,770 feet (540m) above the desert. Between them run cleft valleys, some as narrow as crevices.

In 1872 the explorer Ernest Giles described Kata Tjuta as "rounded minarets, giant cupolas and monstrous domes." He named the whole formation Mount Olga after the

A huge block of
conglomerate rocks lies
below Kala Tjuta, which
means "many heads."

From Uluru one can
see across the desert
to Kata Tjuta.

Uluru, which means "mother
of the earth," rises abruptly
over the red desert sand in
the center of Australia.

Spanish queen. That same year, Uluru was "discovered" by William Gosse, who on the same trip climbed to its highest point. Gosse named the massif Ayers Rock, after a South Australian politician who had supported him. In his diary Gosse wrote that the rock is "the most wonderful natural feature I have ever seen."

In this way the rocks acquired their famous Western names, but in 1985, when the national park was handed back to its indigenous inhabitants, these landmarks were officially given the Aboriginal names of Uluru and Kata Tjuta. And today the Australian State leases the area from the Aborigines, who look after the national park in collaboration with the nature conservation authorities.

Uluru can be freely translated as "mother of the earth" and Kata Tjuta means "many heads." Both massifs are sacred to the Anangu Aborigines, who have lived here for 20,000 years. On rock slabs ancient cave paintings can be seen. According to legend, Uluru was created by two boys who carved the mountain out of soil that had softened in the rain. The holes and pits in the rock are held to be the scars of battles between animal-like ancestors. That is not a bad explanation.

ULURU–
KATA TJUTA

REGISTERED: 1987. Natural
and cultural heritage.
COUNTRY: Australia.
(Northern Territory).
FORM OF CONSERVATION:
National park.
CRITERIA: Ecology, natural beauty.
SIZE: 510 square miles
(1,325sq km).
ALTITUDE: 1,115–2,830 feet
(340–862m) above sea level.
LANDSCAPE: Two isolated massifs
19 miles (30km) apart. Uluru is
about 2 miles (3.5km) long and
1 mile (2km) wide, rising to
1,150 feet (350m). Kata Tjuta
forms 36 steep rock domes
with short valleys and clefts.
The surrounding desert has
low dunes of reddish sand.
VEGETATION: Open areas with
scattered trees and bushes
alternate with denser stands
of trees. The flora is typical
of central Australia, with 390
species of vascular plants.
Grassy tussocks all year round,
but some plants only exist
for a short time after the rains.
FAUNA: 3 large mammals:
dingoes, giant red kangaroos,
and rock-based wallaroos,
found only at Kata Tjuta. Several
small marsupials, rodents, and
bats are active at night. Around
66 resident bird species.
Several common, large,
poisonous snakes, including the
deadly brown snake.
CULTURAL HISTORY: Uluru has
great sacred significance
for the Aborigines. Both massifs
are at the crossroads of
Aboriginal "songlines."
CONSERVATION VALUE: The rocks are
unique natural phenomena and
the deserts are representative
of the interior of Australia. The
Aborigines' way of life has
developed symbiotically with
the ecology of the region.
TOURISM: 500,000 visitors
per year.

TASMANIA

—THE WILDERNESS ISLAND

There are nine unique species of the pandani grass tree.

The slopes of Mount Hayes (3,410 feet/1,040m) have impenetrable vegetation.

Following pages: Lake Oberon lies in remote terrain, in a glacial basin in the heart of the Arthur Range.

AT FIRST GLANCE the landscape of western Tasmania reminds us of northern Europe. It has extensive areas of wilderness and gentle, measured contours, which during our journey on one of the few roads in the area makes the atmosphere feel just like home. We see the forest spreading out like a sultry taiga, and in the background there are long, moderately high mountains, like distant blue stage curtains.

But on closer inspection the landscape offers a more exotic experience. We walk along a path cut through a tangle of intertwined tree trunks. All around, trees grow like spillikins, making the forest completely inaccessible, and the few upright trees are only 30 feet (10m) high. However, Tasmania also has forests that are ideal for walking in, such as groves of pencil pines, which are thought to be a remnant from the continent of Gondwanaland. Another type of Tasmanian forest contains swamp gum (*Eucalyptus regnans*), the world's tallest deciduous tree, reaching almost 311 feet (95m).

Although the mountains look familiar from a distance, they too are an alien environment. The bedrock consists of pale-colored quartzites and dolomites, 750 million years old. A system of ridges runs north-south across the island and between them lie lowland strips. The land is marshy and difficult to walk on, and thigh-high tussock grass dominates where there are no trees or bush. During our walk we keep to the paths, even in open country—it is virtually impossible to do otherwise.

During the Ice Age, Tasmania's mountains received a face-lift. Small glaciers were created, which carved out contoured basins in the sides of the mountains. When the ice had disappeared the basins were exposed—typical examples are those in the Arthur Range. The broken relief of this mountain chain looks like the work of a giant, who pressed his thumb down into the mountain at regular intervals, and each imprint became a small, delicate lake now filled from a stream. Here it is as if we are on a rollercoaster going over pass after pass, from lake to lake, as we travel through a furrowed, mountain landscape that exudes the elegant beauty of maturity.

Yet the most unusual aspect of Tasmania's landscape is its unique fauna. The legendary Tasmanian tiger—the island's biggest predator, almost the size of a small wolf—may still lurk in the bush. During the first half of the twentieth century this marsupial was decimated by sheep farmers and the last recorded sighting was in 1946.

The characteristic cushiony
growth of *Abrotanella* forms
clumps 3 feet (1m) wide.

The rugged mountains in
the South West National
Park seen from 3,345-foot
(1,020m) high Mount Orion.

However, unconfirmed sightings suggest that it may live on in inaccessible corners. Another strange (and, paradoxically, timid) carnivorous marsupial is the Tasmanian devil, which is the size of a hare and looks more ferocious than it really is. During our walk we encounter the deadly poisonous tiger snake, which is more prolific in Tasmania than on the Australian mainland.

In the nineteenth century the island was plundered by loggers and gold-prospectors; and at the same time the Aborigines finally died out. One of the pioneers—William Tully—loved "the river scenery with its rugged outline, and the tortuous ravines," and in 1859 he made his way to the Franklin River, which tumbles through a long, deep gorge. This river became world famous in 1982, when plans to turn it into a source of hydroelectric power were drawn up, just as the area had achieved the status of a World Heritage site. Australia's supreme court then decided that the project was illegal in view of the country's undertaking to protect the area and the river was saved. Some ten years previously, the island's most beautiful lake had been allowed to be spoiled but, on the whole, western Tasmania is one of the remaining genuine wildernesses of the world.

TASMANIA

REGISTERED: 1982, natural and cultural heritage.

COUNTRY: Australia.

FORM OF CONSERVATION: 5 national parks, 3 state parks, 4 nature conservation areas, 3 forest reserves, 1 game reserve, and a biosphere reserve.

CRITERIA: Geology, ecology, natural beauty, and threatened species.

SIZE: 5,340 square miles (13,836sq km).

ALTITUDE: 0–5,350 feet (0–1,617m) above sea level.

LANDSCAPE: Mountain chains of primary rock from north to south. Peaks shaped by Ice Age glaciers. Deep river valleys. Rocky coastline with lagoons.

VEGETATION: Over half the area is moorland. Temperate rainforest covers another third. Scrub and grass grow on bare ground, and half the species are endemic.

FAUNA: 4 types of marsupial, including the Tasmanian devil. Of 150 bird species, 13 are indigenous. 11 species of reptile, of which 4 are endemic.

CULTURAL HISTORY: Aborigines lived here prior to the Ice Age 12,000 years ago when rising waters isolated the land. About 30 ancient caves, once inhabited; many paintings. Tasmania's first prison was built on the coast.

CONSERVATION VALUE: The largest wilderness in Australia's temperate territory. Big range of natural environments and exceptional numbers of endemic plants and animals.

TOURISM: 200,000 visitors per year.

—A GIANT BIOLOGICAL MARVEL

The first Europeans to land on Heron Island in 1843 were impressed by the large number of reef herons.

Heron Island lies on the leeward side of the reef, where currents deposit coral sand. This fragile, "Robinson Crusoe" isle can only cope with a maximum of 250 visitors per day.

A TREMENDOUS UNDERWATER FORTRESS, almost an organic version of the Great Wall of China, is how we might describe the Great Barrier Reef. According to astronauts it is the only living formation on Earth that can be seen from the moon. Flying over the reef gave us some idea—it looks like a multicolored carpet. In the transparent sea turquoise areas alternate with dark patches and garlands of coral strips.

We fly to the tiny paradise isle of Heron Island, named after the white herons that disport themselves here. The island is remote, lying in the open sea 44 miles (70km) from the Australian mainland, and is part of the Capricorn archipelago. Heron Island was formed from coral fragments that the waves broke off and ground to sand. In the center is dense tropical forest, while the periphery is bare. Along the short stretches of beach there are soft rocks where phosphate from bird droppings has cemented the sand and turned it black.

In the dawn light we search for egg-laying turtles. The beaches of the Great Barrier Reef are an important breeding ground for six of the world's seven turtle species, but the number of females that come varies from year to year, depending on climatic variations. The humpback whale also breeds here, in the water inside the outer reef. The beds of sea grass provide food for herds of globally threatened dugongs—the real creatures on which mermaids are thought to be based.

When the ebb tide exposes the reef, we can walk cautiously out to sea. The rough surface of the reef projects only slightly above the lapping water and the coral spreads as far as the eye can see, like a stony, wet desert. The scenery creates an odd impression—we don't quite know whether it is land or sea.

The reef is formed not only from billions of tiny coral creatures, but also from small algae. Recently, water pollution and rising sea temperatures have bleached the coral. It is also destroyed by a natural enemy—the starfish *Acanthaster*. Sometimes found in colonies a million strong, the starfish feeds ravenously on the polyps. The reef recovers about ten years after such an attack. According to one theory this phenomenon is a form of biological renewal comparable to forest fires.

The Great Barrier Reef is actually a composite network of coral reefs of different sizes. Some are less than two-and-a-half acres (1ha) in size, while others cover an area

Dawn casts a magical light
on the beach of Heron
Island at high tide.

Sea perch like
to congregate in the
waters around the reef.

At low tide one can walk out
on the two-million-year-old
Great Barrier Reef.

An egg-laying turtle
lingers on the beach
at daybreak.

of more than 38 square miles (100sq km). At its highest it rises 395 feet (120m) above its base, which consists of prehistoric and dead reefs. The fastest growth occurs in clear, clean water out toward the Pacific Ocean. The whole biological structure is huge, covering an area larger than Great Britain, but the corals comprise only 5 percent of the seabed. Between the outer reefs and the mainland lies the Great Barrier Reef Lagoon—a large shallow sea on the continental shelf.

The waters here are highly treacherous for sailors and the large number of wrecks is testament to the number of ships lost in all weathers. Perhaps thirty of the wrecks are of historical interest. Of course, the most exciting part of this outstanding marine environment is underwater. Surrounded by an apparently limitless horizon, we dive down to the reef and see all manner of fish swim past. The coral structure is a disorienting three-dimensional world and in the cavities between the hard surfaces live myriad plants and molluscs. The biodiversity of the reef is often compared to that of the tropical rainforests and, taking the analogy further, the Great Barrier Reef can be described as the "Amazon of the seas."

GREAT BARRIER REEF

REGISTERED: 1981.
COUNTRY: Australia (Queensland).
FORM OF CONSERVATION: Marine
national park.
CRITERIA: Geology, ecology, natural
beauty, threatened species.
SIZE: 134,632 square miles
(348,700sq km).
ALTITUDE: Seabed—150 feet (40m)
above sea level.
LANDSCAPE: About 1,250-mile
(2,000km) long system of coral
reefs; 3,400 separate reefs and 300
coral islands. Between the reefs are
600 islands with firm bedrock.

Where currents are strong, coral
grows freestanding; elsewhere,
as border reefs along the rocks.
VEGETATION: The coral islands have
a unique forest with cabbage palms,
pandanus, and fig. On the mainland,
dense rainforest on the seaward
slopes. Mangrove forests cover
shallow creeks and bays. Meadows
of seaweed and sea grass beneath
the ocean's surface.
FAUNA: More than 400 different
species of coral animals on the
reef. A multitude of marine animals,
15,000 fish species, 4,000 mollusk

species. One of the world's largest
populations of dugongs and turtles.
250 bird species nest in the area.
CULTURAL HISTORY: Aborigines
inhabited the area for thousands
of years. The northern coast is
important for its cave paintings.
CONSERVATION VALUE: The world's
largest coral reef with outstanding
biodiversity and innumerable
natural environments for threatened
species. Marine landscape of
great beauty.
TOURISM: 2.5 million visitors
per year.

FRASER ISLAND
—RAINFOREST ON SAND

The island has a strong population of unusually purebred dingoes—Australian wild dogs.

Fraser Island belongs to the east coast's Great Sandy Regions where Australia's rivers have distributed sand over a huge area.

WE TRUDGE OVER A MINIATURE DESERT framed by dense forest. Up on the highest dune we see the ocean shining beyond a green curtain. In less than an hour we have completely switched natural environments.

The almost straight beach that stretches for 75 miles (120km) along the eastern side of Fraser Island is one of Australia's longest, undeveloped beaches. At low tide the beach is like a 330-feet (100m) wide landing strip that is used by all-terrain vehicles, but at high water it is inaccessible. In 1836 Captain James Fraser was shipwrecked in the long shallows offshore. When the crew reached land they met hostile Aborigines who called the island "K'gari"—paradise. However, Matthew Flinder, who sailed around Australia in 1803, recorded that "nothing could be more barren than this peninsula."

But Fraser Island is neither odd nor barren. There are several small lakes and the interior of the island is covered with wonderful forests. The island has the world's only rainforest that grows on sand, along the watercourses. The satinay tree, which reaches a height of up to 195 feet (60m), is a species found only here. Together with brush boxwood and the common eucalyptus species, the satinay was felled by the timber industry for 130 years until finally, in 1992, the forests were protected. The last Aborigines had disappeared long before, but their paradise was eventually saved.

FRASER ISLAND

REGISTERED: 1992.

COUNTRY: Australia (Queensland).

FORM OF CONSERVATION: National park.

CRITERIA: Ecology, natural beauty.

SIZE: 641 square miles (1,662sq km).

ALTITUDE: 0–785 feet (0–240m) above sea level.

LANDSCAPE: Island 75 miles (120km) long and 3–15 miles (5–25km) wide, with sand dunes of differing ages. In hollows formed by the wind there are about 40 unique lakes fed by the island's large groundwater reservoir. The sand extends 195 feet (60m) beneath the surface of the sea.

VEGETATION: Vegetation zoning across the island. 13 square miles (33sq km) covered by rainforest. The biggest dunes have tall eucalyptus forest. Mangrove swamps along the side of the island that faces the mainland.

FAUNA: Purebred dingoes, a rich reptile fauna, and a large number of frog species. Remarkably few introduced animal species. Over 200 species of birds.

CULTURAL HISTORY: Aborigines came to the island 2,000 years ago, but the sand has preserved few archaeological remains.

CONSERVATION VALUE: The world's largest sand island. Unique rainforest that grows on sand, and freshwater lakes.

TOURISM: 300,000 visitors per year.

WET TROPICS
—A REMNANT OF GONDWANALAND

This stick insect is superbly adapted to the forest environment.

The ancient rainforest in the Wet Tropics has examples of flora illustrating many stages of evolution.

Following pages: Tree ferns can be traced back to the dawn of history, and even to the age of dinosaurs.

WHAT A WEALTH OF PLANTS, in terms of both species and evolution! This is the bewildering impression of Wet Tropics, the fertile World Heritage site humming with activity on Queensland's beautiful coast. The site is composed of more than fifty national parks and other reserves, and covers a huge area. We are carried over the mountain ridges and the rainforest in the Barron Falls Gorge National Park by a cable railway—reputedly the longest in the world. There are no scars of human activity visible in the rainforest beneath us. Environmentalists protested against the construction of the railway, but as the forest has no roads, and the only other form of access is by helicopter, the cable railway has come to be accepted by even the most ardent environmentalists.

It is humid down in the forest. Proud trunks carry the canopy high above the bushy undergrowth where Ulysses butterflies float by on deep blue wings. On the forest floor fungi, lichen, and mosses mount a colorful attack on leaves, stumps, and fallen, rotten tree trunks, turning them back into soil. A few lianas are noticeable, as they strangle the life out of their host trees and seek nourishment in the thin layer of earth through their hanging roots. The ancient forest is like a Gothic cathedral, with decorated columns and well-preserved foliage frescoes on the domed ceiling of the cupola. There are unique animals and birds here, such as Lumholtz's southern tree kangaroo and the cassowary—a flightless bird that lives on the ground—as well as snakes and frogs.

Near a huge ravine we glimpse the 860-foot (265m) high Barron Falls through the trees. And today the falls are only a trickle compared with the force they had until 1935, when a power station was built here. The artist Ellis Rowan traveled here at the end of the nineteenth century to capture with her paintbrush flowers hitherto unknown in the West. Rowan described the forest at Barron River as "a network of branches, all hung and festooned with thickets of clematis, convulvulus, and flowering begonias, erythrinas, tossing acacias, feathery palms."

The readily accessible national park constitutes just a fraction of the Wet Tropics World Heritage area. We continue north in a four-wheel-drive vehicle across the coastal forests along grit roads beside the Daintree and Bloomfield rivers, and walk in the national parks of Daintree, Cape Tribulation, Cedar Bay, and Black Mountain. At Cape Tribulation the rainforest runs right out to the headland, which got its name from

At Cape Tribulation the rainforest runs right down to the Pacific coast.

Wet Tropics is home to almost half of Australia's birds, including these red-tailed black cockatoos.

Tjapukai Aborigines own and run a cultural center close to the rainforest.

Black Mountain is made up of huge granite boulders.

William Hann's expedition to the York Peninsula in 1872: "There was not even a ghost of a chance of finding a path to enter this labyrinthine maze and to try to force our way through it would have been madness."

At the northernmost tip of the World Heritage site is Black Mountain—a hill sacred to the Aborigines. It is not a rock, but a huge mound of stones. The hill consists of enormous, stacked, granite blocks that have been polished smooth by a black lichen, making the whole hill appear black. Several unique species of lizard live here.

We catch a glimpse of Bloomfield Falls, then the rainforest closes in around us. The darkness of the rainforest conceals more than 3,000 species of higher plants, of which almost 1,200 are trees, and more than fifty threatened or rare species of vertebrates. This rainforest has living examples that represent the main stages in the history of evolution, from the era of ferns to coniferous trees and cone-bearing palm trees to flowering vascular plants. It is thought that the rainforest is a relic from the supercontinent Gondwanaland, which provided the nursery for eucalyptus and other genera to evolve before they spread over the Australian continent when the climate became drier.

WET TROPICS

REGISTERED: 1988.

COUNTRY: Australia (Queensland).

FORM OF CONSERVATION: 19 national parks, 36 forest reserves.

CRITERIA: Geology, ecology, natural beauty, threatened species.

SIZE: 3,450 square miles (8,944sq km).

ALTITUDE: 0–5,320 feet (0–1,622m) above sea level.

LANDSCAPE: Coastal lowland broken up by escarpments with many ravines and waterfalls; tableland with the Great Divide range. Coral reefs offshore.

VEGETATION: 13 types of rainforest. On the mountain, low-growing trees with a dense canopy; in the lowland, taller trees overgrown with lianas and ferns; in the west, open forest with eucalyptus and acacia; on the coast, mangrove swamps. More than 3,000 species of vascular plants,

FAUNA: 54 species of vertebrates, including 9 mammals found only in this area. 4 species of ring-tailed opossum, 2 of tree kangaroo, 33 of bat, and over 370 bird species. On the tableland 13 endemic bird species, 47 species of native frogs, 160 species of reptiles.

CULTURAL HISTORY: Aborigines have lived here for over 40,000 years in the world's oldest rainforest culture.

CONSERVATION VALUE: Varied, natural beauty, ancient rainforest with flora in many stages of evolution.

TOURISM: 4.8 million visitors per year.

TONGARIRO

—COLORFUL VOLCANOES

Trekking up the slopes of the spectacular Red Crater.

The volcanoes on the North Island lie along the frontier between two of the Earth's tectonic plates. Ngauruhoe rises above the Red Crater.

THE POPULAR TREKKERS' PATH, Tongariro Crossing, leads into a volcanic landscape so colorful that it looks unreal. The eruptions have "painted" the sterile landscape and created a gallery of earth-based palettes. From the edge of the evocatively named Red Crater rise rock walls of brittle and weathered scorial lava—a variant of the basalt that is thrown up onto the volcanic cone. Usually this lava is gray or black but here it has oxidized to a blood-red shade, and in some places to a chocolate-brown.

The Tongariro volcanic massif rises majestically in the middle of New Zealand's North Island. Since time immemorial these mountains have been symbols of the Maoris' identity and spirit—*mana*. In 1885 Chief Tukino IV expressed his concern that the Europeans would claim them: "Tongariro is my ancestor, my *tupuna*; it is my head, my *mana* centers around Tongariro. My father's bones lie here today. After I am dead what will be their fate?" He wanted to prevent the land being broken up and sold into private ownership and gave Tongariro to New Zealand's people. Ten years later the British Crown designated the area a national park, the fourth in the world.

The botanist John Bidwill had attracted the wrath of the Maoris in 1839 when he became the first European to climb Ngauruhoe, which at 7,515 feet (2,291m) high is the most symmetrical of the volcanoes in the massif. After that trip he wrote that the crater was a menacing abyss. He stated that all the sides were overhanging and the vapors prevented him from seeing the bottom. Today, as we climb the steep, 1,968-feet (600m) high, north side, we come to two crater hollows—a small one inside a larger one measuring a couple of hundred yards across. Ngauruhoe forms an evenly tapering stratus volcano, just 2,500 years old. It used to have powerful eruptions of ash every nine years, but the cycle has now been broken and there have been none since 1975.

In the Red Crater we are dumbfounded by its grandeur and the strange shapes. Activity in this volcano began 10,000 years ago and after a period of violent eruptions the whole mountain exploded. One of the lava channels formed a pipe which then caved in and it now has the shape of a pair of breasts in the middle of the rock wall.

Farther on new color sensations await us. We pass bright yellow patches of sulfur deposits and reach the Emerald Lakes—two vivid, green pools that have acquired their color from mineral seepage. These miniature lakes are toxic and they are also cold even

The Emerald Lakes are just as toxic as they look.

Fumaroles and sulfur springs are found on the volcanoes.

Ketetahi Springs is one of the area's three hot springs.

though hot steam rises from holes in the surrounding scree. Next, we go up to the Blue Lake Crater, where yet another color is added to the palette. This crater has a basin filled with water as blue as ink.

South of Tongariro stands the national park's biggest and most active volcano, Ruapehu, 9,175 feet (2,797m) high. On the north side there is a skiing center, which continues to operate in spite of the fact that the volcano has erupted six times since 1945. The volcano is explosive because of its gaseous andesite magma, containing sulfur dioxide. Permanent ice fields cover the top part, and down in the crater lies a warm-water lake. When there is an eruption the lake can overflow and send mud-streams or lahars down the slopes. In 1953, an eruption caused a lahar that crushed the railway bridge at Tangiwai just before an express train went through, and 151 people died.

East of the volcano lies a barren lava desert and between them is a col where European heather thrives. It was planted in the 1920s to sustain introduced grouse, but fortunately the project was halted. Although the ecology of the area has been affected, the colorful landscape has been largely preserved, just as Chief Tukino IV wished.

TONGARIRO

REGISTERED: 1988. Additionally as a cultural heritage site 1993.

COUNTRY: New Zealand (North Island).

FORM OF CONSERVATION: National park.

CRITERIA: Ecology, natural beauty.

SIZE: 310 square miles (796sq km).

ALTITUDE: 1,640–9,745 feet (500–2,970m) above sea level.

LANDSCAPE: Chain of volcanoes with inactive volcanic peaks in the north and 3 active volcanoes in the south. These consist of cones, craters, explosion pits, lava flows, and crater lakes. The lava is andesite.

Hot sulfur springs discharge gases. 15,000 years ago, the ice formed troughs and moraine walls.

VEGETATION: Below 3,280 feet (1,000m) in the northwest there are pockets of rainforest with *Podocarpus* trees. Above this there is beech forest with species of *Nothofagus*. Large areas of land with grass, brush, and bushes. Gravel and boulders predominate at the highest levels. West of the mountains is a desert of red-brown sand.

FAUNA: New Zealand's only indigenous vertebrates are birds and 2 bat species. 56 bird species observed in the area, including several threatened species, such as the brown kiwi. Introduced species include stoats, feral cats, hares, possums, and red deer.

CULTURAL HISTORY: Of great religious and cultural significance to the Maori people.

CONSERVATION VALUE: Volcanoes with frequent eruptions. Various ecosystems typical of the North Island on the slopes .

TOURISM: 1 million visitors per year.

FIORDLAND

—WHERE MOUNTAINS MEET THE SEA

The kea or mountain parrot
is fearless and often seen
along the Milford Track.

Kayaks in the fiord of
Doubtful Sound, seen here
on a typical day, with the
mountains shrouded in rain.

Following pages: The
stunning view from
Mackinnon Pass (3,520 feet/
1,073m) down into
Arthur's Valley.

WE FOLLOW A ONE-WAY PATH. This sounds ridiculous, but it means that because there is nobody coming toward us we can experience the landscape without disturbance. A maximum of eighty people per day are allowed to go on walking tours here and they all have to go in the same direction. The Milford Track is one of the world's most attractive hiking trails and without this arrangement there would be crowding and erosion.

During the four-day hike we become well acquainted with Fiordland, which is part of Te Wahipounamu—the Maori name for southwestern New Zealand. This area is now an enormous World Heritage site that extends 186 miles (300km) north to Mount Cook, the highest mountain of this island country. In Fiordland, the landscape is particularly inhospitable and there are inaccessible pockets where no man has yet set foot—no mean attribute for a national park in our time. There are tree species that are among the oldest flowering plants on Earth, and the forest provides us with living examples of the vegetation that covered Gondwanaland eighty million years ago.

The valleys are deeply incised and sheltered by steep mountainsides. The vegetation is supported by one of the Earth's wettest climates, with rain falling on 200 days a year. From the coast narrow fiords penetrate inland between the mountains. The first seal-hunters and whalers believed that the fiords opened up on the landward side and called them "sounds." The most dramatic example is Milford Sound, with Mitre Peak mountain, which shoots up from the sea like a pillar to heaven. Even though the top is "only" 5,550 feet (1,692m) high, we have to crane our necks to see the summit. Mitre Peak is a symbol of Fiordland—a region that has the world's highest coastal cliffs.

At the end of the 1870s the Scot Donald Sutherland searched for a trail from Milford Sound to the inhabited area around Te Anua Lake, east of the mountains. However, the route was eventually opened up by two other pioneers who came from the opposite direction across the mountain yoke between Arthur's and Clinton's valleys. Mackinnon Pass was named after one of them. And thus they laid the foundation for the hiking trail known as the Milford Track.

Fiordland had received New Zealand's first European immigrants long before the nineteenth century. Abel Tasman viewed the area in 1642, and more than a century later James Cook anchored in Dusky Sound, where there began a barbaric seal-hunting

Fur seals greet a passing canoeist.

The Milford Track passes Mackay's Waterfall, which nestles deep in the dense rainforest.

industry that decimated the fur seal population. After Fiordland was granted protection in 1904 the seal stocks increased and today there are some 50,000 animals in the fiords.

Another successful recovery has been that of the takahe—a dark blue, flightless rail that was rediscovered in 1948, after not having been seen for fifty years. An intensive rescue campaign began and now there are about 120 birds here. With the immigrants came several non-native species, which have created ecological problems. The stoat threatens birds, and ungulates such as red deer, wapiti, chamois, goats, and wild boar destroy the vegetation. In order to keep stocks down, these species can be hunted freely in the national parks.

A thousand years before the Europeans, the Maoris explored Fiordland in their large, double canoes. They believed that the sea god had created the fiords using huge blocks of stone. In the north of the region they searched for takiwai—a prized type of jade used in jewelry. As we paddle our kayak up Doubtful Sound we see the place from their perspective. The fiord is an enormous basin and we can only land where the rivers have built up banks of sediment. Fiordland is a truly magnificent and impassable area.

FIORDLAND

REGISTERED: 1986, extended 1990.

COUNTRY: New Zealand
(South Island).

FORM OF CONSERVATION: 4 national
parks, 2 nature reserves,
13 protected landscape areas,
4 game reserves.

CRITERIA: Geology, ecology,
natural beauty, threatened
species.

SIZE: 10,000 square miles
(26,000sq km).

ALTITUDE: 0–12,350 feet
(0–3,764m) above sea level.

LANDSCAPE: 30-mile (50km) long
mountain chain with highest
peaks in the north—19 are
over 9,840 feet (3,000m). The
highest mountain, Mount Cook,
is surrounded by several big
glaciers. The southern part is
called Fiordland and has fiords
in the west and alpine lakes in
the east. High waterfalls.

VEGETATION: Temperate rainforest
in the valleys with southern
beeches and 800-year-old trees
of the genus *Podocarpus*. Tree
ferns common. Forest covers
two thirds of the area; in the
east there is brush and grass
vegetation. Above the treeline,
plant-rich heaths and meadows.
Of more than 700 species of
vascular plants, 25 are endemic.

FAUNA: In the fiords: dolphins,
New Zealand fur seals, and the
Fiordland crested penguin.
Several native bird species,
such as two species of kiwi, the
takahe (a giant, flightless rail)
and the kea or mountain parrot.
Introduced species, such as
deer and goats.

CULTURAL HISTORY: The Maoris
lived here for a long time and
have left behind burial caves.

CONSERVATION VALUE: Impressive
mountain landscape with fiords
and deep lakes. Well-developed
temperate rainforest. Shelters
many threatened species.

TOURISM: 450,000 visitors
per year.

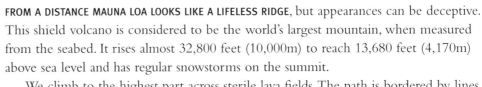

HAWAII VOLCANOES

—NEW LAND IN THE PACIFIC OCEAN

The tough, gaseous
lava pahoehoe sets into
twisted sculptures.

On the coast below Kilauea
the island is being extended
with lava, but the sea
is fighting back.

FROM A DISTANCE MAUNA LOA LOOKS LIKE A LIFELESS RIDGE, but appearances can be deceptive. This shield volcano is considered to be the world's largest mountain, when measured from the seabed. It rises almost 32,800 feet (10,000m) to reach 13,680 feet (4,170m) above sea level and has regular snowstorms on the summit.

We climb to the highest part across sterile lava fields. The path is bordered by lines of black pahoehoe lava that look as though they have been squeezed out of a tube. In one place the path skirts some crater domes that are 30–50 feet (10–15m) high—they bubble with steam and discharge puffs of "smoke" like a dragon.

During the long hike we seem to be drawing closer to a remote peak that looks like the summit, but the silhouette retreats the whole time. Finally, we stand at the rim of the 330-feet (100m) drop—a peephole into the inside of the Earth. Our imaginations run riot even though eruptions can be predicted accurately. Mauna Loa is one of the world's most active volcanoes, having had almost forty eruptions since the mid-nineteenth century. The last occurred in 1984, when a lava flow stopped not far away from Hilo, the island's biggest town.

For a long time the volcanoes on Hawaii were an enigma. Why were they here, so far from the continents? Now we know that the lava originates from a hot spot almost 186 miles (300km) down inside the Earth. The molten material is driven upward and reaches the surface through a fixed "pipe" that passes through both the thick and semiliquid mantles, and the significantly thinner rigid crust. When the magma reaches the seabed it builds up an underwater volcano on the Pacific plate. As this plate is shifting northwest at about 4 inches (10cm) per year, the volcano moves slowly away from the hot spot at the same time as it grows into an island. Finally, the connection is broken and the lava flow becomes dormant. Only a few of the world's active volcanoes are formed and extinguished in this way—for example Loihi, which lies 19 miles (30km) out to sea, and will become a new island in around 200,000 years' time. When James Cook landed on Hawaii in 1778 he found a young country—unknown to the rest of the world even though Polynesians had lived there for a thousand years.

The Hawaii Volcanoes National Park is on Hawaii—the biggest island in the archipelago. Below Mauna Loa there is Kilauea, 4,100 feet (1,248m) high, a hyperactive

volcano with an oval crater. There is nothing in the flat landscape to forewarn of this deep hollow surrounded by vertical walls. Down at the bottom is another crater called Halemaumau, which, according to local legend, is where the fire goddess Pele resides. In her honor the Polynesians erected a stone temple, and there was once a boiling lava lake in the crater, into which people were thrown alive as sacrifices. In 1983 the lava flows opened a new hole almost 12 miles (20km) from Kilauea's crater. At the new site a little volcanic cone formed, and it has been erupting almost continuously ever since.

Because of its height Mauna Loa attracts a lot of precipitation, which waters the subtropical rainforest on the eastern slopes of the volcano. Large treelike ferns lend the vegetation a primeval air—a real Jurassic Park. Isolation has turned Hawaii into a biological laboratory of the same type as the Galápagos Islands. From about 300 original plants, a flora comprising more than a thousand species has developed. Sixteen species of land birds have, over time, become fifty. But because of human activity Hawaii has lost more species than anywhere else on Earth. The list of threatened plants and animals is long and the national park offers those that are left the possibility of survival.

HAWAII VOLCANOES

REGISTERED: 1987.

COUNTRY: USA (Hawaii).

FORM OF CONSERVATION: National park, biosphere reserve.

CRITERIA: Ecology.

SIZE: 360 square miles (929sq km).

ALTITUDE: 0–13,680 feet (4,169m) above sea level.

LANDSCAPE: Comprises two of the world's most active volcanoes. The biggest, Mauna Loa, is a textbook example of a flat-shield volcano. The lower volcano, Kilauea, regularly produces new lava flows.

VEGETATION: Varies from subtropical rainforest with many tree ferns to dry lava deserts with unique plants. The height discrepancy between the sea and the alpine levels with the consequent climatic differences produces major variations in vegetation. More than 90% of the vascular plants are endemic.

FAUNA: Only 2 native mammals: monk seals and bats. Wild boar, mongoose, feral cats and dogs have been introduced. Many bird species have been eradicated, including all the flightless birds, and many others are threatened, such as the Hawaiian goose and a number of Hawaiian honeycreepers.

CULTURAL HISTORY: Rich in relics of Polynesian culture. There are remains of temples, sacred sites, cave paintings, and landing places for canoes.

CONSERVATION VALUE: A unique example of volcanic island formation. The area includes an originally subtropical rainforest with threatened species. Outstanding examples of natural genus evolution caused by volcanic activity.

TOURISM: 2.5 million visitors per year.

"OUR MAGNIFICENT WILDERNESS" IS AN ENVIRONMENTAL PROJECT focused on World Heritage sites. Our aim was to produce the book in an environmentally friendly way in order to fit in with the United Nations' (UN) and World Wildlife Fund's (WWF) global nature conservation concept. Whenever possible we traveled as ecotourists and in choosing the people we worked with we insisted on good environmental credentials. The following have helped us with this project:

CANON, through its environmental declarations on its products, internal environmental training, and well thought-out environmental management system, has shown that it has control over the environmental impact of its business and has therefore been awarded environmental certification in Sweden. The company supports WWF International and is helping it to set up a wildlife picture archive on the Internet. We used Canon equipment for all the small format photography.

FUJIFILM has also received environmental certification for its comprehensive environmental system. Fujifilm's Green Card is its own environmental diploma awarded to photo shops that fulfil their environmental responsibilities. The pictures in the book were mainly taken with Fujichrome Velvia slide film.

PROLABBET in Stockholm developed all the films. It was among the first of Sweden's professional photo laboratories to invest in far-reaching environmental adaptation to comply with the requirements of the new Environmental Code. Cleaning and collection systems for chemicals, closed recycling systems for bleaching baths, and stringent control of the rinsing water are some of the measures that have been adopted.

STORA ENSO FINE PAPER produces at its Grycksbo Mill the environmentally certified Multi Art Matt paper which is used in this book. Stora Enso hold quality and environmental certificates in accordance with international standards. They also carry out environmental reviews of their wood suppliers and sub-contractors.

WWF SWEDEN supported the project morally throughout and later chose it as the Panda Book of the Year 2001. With its well-known commitment to the conservation of natural environments around the world, WWF was a natural collaborator. It also has a system called Global 200 for supporting environmental conservation in many countries around the world. WWF International and Canon are working together on a digital photo library.

We would like to thank all who have contributed—organizations, companies, and private individuals.

The authors

THE AUTHORS ARE RESPONSIBLE FOR ALL IMAGES AND TEXT IN THEIR RESPECTIVE CHAPTERS, AS FOLLOWS:

CLAES GRUNDSTEN: CHITWAN, FIORDLAND, FRASER ISLAND, GRAND CANYON, THE GREAT BARRIER REEF, HAWAII VOLCANOES, KEOLADEO GHANA, KILIMANJARO, LAPONIA, MOUNT KENYA, NANDA DEVI, NGORONGORO, THE PYRENEES, SAGARMATHA, SERENGETI, TASMANIA, TONGARIRO, TSINGY BEMARAHA, ULURU–KATA TJUTA, WATERTON GLACIER, YOSEMITE PLUS PAGES 85, 101, 155, 184–5 AND THE SPINE IMAGE (TIGER IN INDIA).

PETER HANNEBERG: ALDABRA, ALTAI MOUNTAINS, DOÑANA, EVERGLADES, GALÁPAGOS, GUANACASTE, IGUAÇU/IGUAZÚ, KAKADU, KAZIRANGA, LOS GLACIARES, MANA POOLS, REDWOOD, THE ROCKY MOUNTAINS, TIKAL, VALDÉS PENINSULA, VALLÉE DE MAI, VICTORIA FALLS, WET TROPICS, YELLOWSTONE PLUS PAGES 9, 47, 181 AND THE COVER PICTURE (MORAINE LAKE, THE ROCKY MOUNTAINS, CANADA).

UNESCO'S NATURAL HERITAGE SITES 2002

(B) = DENOTES THAT THIS SITE IS ALSO A BIOSPHERE RESERVE UNDER UNESCO'S MAN AND THE BIOSPHERE PROGRAM (MAB)
(C) = DENOTES THAT THIS SITE IS ONE OF MIXED NATURAL AND CULTURAL HERITAGE

NORTH AMERICA

1. Kluane, Glacier Bay etc. (B), Canada–USA
2. Nahanni, Canada
3. Wood Buffalo, Canada
4. Dinosaur, Canada
5. The Rocky Mountains, Canada
6. Waterton Glacier (B), Canada–USA
7. Miguasha, Canada
8. Gros Morne, Canada
9. Olympic (B), USA
10. Redwood (B), USA
11. Yosemite, USA
12. Grand Canyon, USA
13. Yellowstone (B), USA
14. Carlsbad Caverns, USA
15. Great Smoky Mountains (B), USA
16. Mammoth Cave (B), USA
17. Everglades (B), USA
18. El Vizcaino (B), Mexico
19. Desembarco del Granma, Cuba
20. Alejandro de Humboldt, Cuba
21. Morne Trois Pitons, Dominica

SOUTH AMERICA

22. Sian Ka'an (B), Mexico
23. Tikal (B, C) Guatemala
24. Belize Barrier Reef, Belize
25. Rio Plátano (B), Honduras
26. Guanacaste, Costa Rica
27. Cocos Island, Costa Rica
28. Talamanca Range–La Amistad (B), Costa Rica–Panama
29. Darien (B), Panama
30. Los Katios, Colombia
31. Canaima, Venezuela
32. Central Suriname, Suriname
33. Jaú National Park, Brazil
34. Brazilian Atlantic Islands, Brazil
35. Galápagos (B), Ecuador
36. Sangay, Ecuador
37. Rio Abiseo (C), Peru
38. Huascarán (B), Peru
39. Machu Picchu (C), Peru
40. Manú (B), Peru
41. Noel Kempff Mercado, Bolivia
42. Cerrado (B), Brazil
43. Discovery Coast, Brazil
44. Atlantic Forest, Brazil
45a. Iguaçu, Brazil
45b. Iguazú, Argentina
46. Pantanal, Brazil
47. Ischigualasto–Talampaya, Argentina
48. Valdés Peninsula, Argentina
49. Los Glaciares, Argentina

EUROPE

50. Laponia (C), Sweden
51. The High Coast, Sweden
52. Bialowieza(B), Poland–Byelorussia
53. St. Kilda (B), Great Britain
54. Causeway Coast, Great Britain
55. Dorset and East Devon Coast, Great Britain
56. Messel Pit Fossil, Germany
57. The Pyrenees (B, C), Spain–France
58. Doñana (B), Spain
59. Madeiras laurel forest, Portugal
60. Ibiza (C), Spain
61. Cape Girolata etc., France
62. Jungfrau–Aletsch–Bietschhorn, Switzerland
63. Skocjan Caves, Slovenia
64. Aggtelek etc. (B), Hungary–Slovakia
65. Danube Delta (B), Romania
66. Plitvice, Croatia
67. Aeolian Islands, Italy
68. Durmitor (B), Yugoslavia
69. Ohrid Region (C), Macedonia
70. Srebarna (B), Bulgaria
71. Pirin (B), Bulgaria
72. Mount Athos (C), Greece
73. Meteora (C), Greece
74. Western Caucasus (B), Russia
75. Komi Forest, Russia

AFRICA

76. Ichkeul (B), Tunisia
77. Tassili N'Ajjer (C), Algeria
78. Aïr-Ténéré (B), Niger
79. Garajonay, (Spain)
80. "W" National Park (B), Niger
81. Banc d'Arguin, Mauritania
82. Nikolo–Koba (B), Senegal
83. Djoudj, Senegal
84. Bandiagara (C), Mali
85. Mount Nimba (B), Guinea–Ivory Coast
86. Taï (B), Ivory Coast
87. Comoé (B), Ivory Coast
88. St. Floris etc., Central Africa
89. Simen, Ethiopia
90. Dja (B), Cameroon
91. Garamba, Zaire
92. Okapi Faunal Reserve, Zaire
93. Virunga, Zaire
94. Salonga, Zaire
95. Kahuzi–Biega, Zaire
96. Bwindi, Uganda
97. Ruwenzori, Uganda
98. Sibiloi etc., Kenya
99. Mount Kenya (B), Kenya
100. Serengeti (B), Tanzania
101. Ngorongoro (B), Tanzania
102. Kilimanjaro, Tanzania
103. Selous, Tanzania
104. Vallée de Mai, Seychelles
105. Aldabra, Seychelles
106. Tsingy Bemaraha, Madagascar
107. Lake Malawi, Malawi
108. Victoria Falls, Zambia–Zimbabwe
109. Mana Pools and Sapi–Chewore, Zimbabwe
110. St. Lucia, South Africa
111. Drakensberg (C), South Africa
112. Gough Island, (Great Britain)

ASIA

113. Hierapolis–Pamukkale (C), Turkey
114. Göreme–Cappadocia (C), Turkey
115. Arabian Oryx Sanctuary, Oman
116. Altai Mountains (B), Russian Federation
117. Lake Baikal (B), Russian Federation
118. Kamchatka (B), Russian Federation
119. Central Sikhote–Alin (B), Russian Federation
120. Shirakami–Sanchi, Japan
121. Yakushima (B), Japan
122. Mount Taishan (C), China
123. Mount Juangshan (C), China
124. Mount Wuyi (C), China
125. Wulingyuan, China
126. Jiuzhaigou (B), China
127. Huanglong, China
128. Mount Emei–Leshan (C), China
129. Nanda Devi, India
130. Keoladeo Ghana, India
131. Sundarbans, India
132. Manas, India
133. Kaziranga, India
134. Chitwan, Nepal
135. Sagarmatha, Nepal
136. Sundarbans, Bangladesh
137. Sinharaja (B), Sri Lanka
138. Ha Long Bay, Vietnam
139. Thungyai–Huai Kha Khaeng, Thailand
140. Puerto–Princesa, Philippines
141. Tubbataha Reef (B), Philippines
142. Kinabalu, Malaysia
143. Gunung Mulu, Malaysia
144. Ujung Kulon, Indonesia
145. Komodo (B), Indonesia
146. Lorentz, Indonesia

OCEANIA

147. East Rennel, Solomon Islands
148. Kakadu (C), Australia
149. Fossil Mammal Sites, Australia
150. Wet Tropics, Australia
151. Great Barrier Reef, Australia
152. Fraser Island, Australia
153. Uluru–Kata Tjuta (B, C), Australia
154. Shark Bay, Australia
155. Central Eastern Rainforest, Australia
156. Lord Howe Island, Australia
157. Greater Blue Mountains, Australia
158. Willandra Lakes (C), Australia
159. Heard and McDonald Islands, Australia
160. Macquarie Island (B), Australia
161. Tasmania (B, C), Australia
162. Sub-Antarctic Islands, New Zealand
163. Fiordland, New Zealand
164. Tongariro (C), New Zealand
165. Hawaii Volcanoes (B), USA
166. Henderson Island (Great Britain)

Note: The total number of sites is 167 rather than 166 because Iguaçu (Brazil) and Iguazú (Argentina) counts as one for each country. This list was agreed at UNESCO's meeting in December 2001.